ON THE BALL

Short Stories, Anecdotes, and Words of Wisdom on the Mental Side of Sport

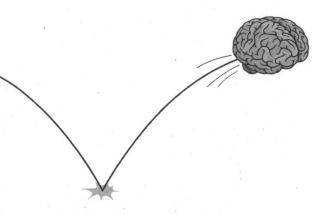

Michael Lodewyks

 FriesenPress

One Printers Way
Altona, MB R0G 0B0
Canada

www.friesenpress.com

ISBN
978-1-03-917814-4 (Hardcover)
978-1-03-917813-7 (Paperback)
978-1-03-917815-1 (eBook)

1. SPORTS & RECREATION, SPORTS PSYCHOLOGY

Distributed to the trade by The Ingram Book Company

KRISTINA,

TAANKS FOR AN AWESOME TIME TODAY ON THE LINKS. ENJOY THE REST OF YOUR TRIP AND I HOPE YOU ENJOY THE BOOK!

MIKE

TABLE OF CONTENTS

AUTHOR'S NOTE

I woke in the middle of the night and could not fall back asleep. Out of boredom, I got up. I was in the middle of my *second* silent meditation retreat and was not allowed to use my phone, read, write, or exercise. Meditation was also out of the question, since I'd be doing that for ten and a half hours the next day.

It was dead quiet. Nothing but empty space.

I began pondering life and the direction I was headed.

Within minutes, I remembered a few words from an athlete I had coached a few years back. She said to me, "You should write a book about this stuff." *This stuff* was referring to the mental skills I introduced to our team that year. At the time she said it, I laughed it off and never thought much more of it. Now, I found it interesting that the comment had resurfaced midway through a meditation retreat, and wouldn't go away. I guess it had lain dormant in my subconscious mind over the past few years and meditating brought it to the surface.

That morning, when we closed our eyes to begin our day of meditation, I had a difficult time concentrating on my breath. My mind kept wandering toward the idea of writing this book. Since I wasn't allowed to write anything down, I began mentally collecting the stories you are about to read. By the end of the day, I had the entire book laid out in my mind and was ready to jump out of my chair in excitement.

When I got home a few days later, the first thing I did was open up my laptop and start feverishly writing.

So here it is, a compilation of my experiences and the wisdom I have gained over many years as an athlete, coach, teacher, and student of the mental side of sport.

INTRODUCTION

As a kid, I loved watching professional sports and was always fascinated by incredible clutch performances. Let me test your memory on a few...

Do you remember "the drive?" When Denver Broncos quarterback John Elway took his team the entire length of the field in the final two minutes of the 1987 AFC championship game? If you don't recall, Elway started the drive on his own two-yard line, with a jersey half-covered in mud. He put together a string of amazing plays with the utmost composure, including two fourth-down conversions. That drive tied the game. The Broncos eventually won in overtime with a few more heroic plays from Elway to get them into field goal range. Crazy!

How about Mark Messier guaranteeing victory prior to game six of the 1994 Eastern Conference Finals? His team, the New York Rangers, was down 3-2 in the series to the New Jersey Devils when he made his guarantee. In game six, the Rangers found themselves down 2-0 and on the brink of elimination. However, Messier scored a hat trick in the third period to win the game. They went on to win the Stanley Cup. Incredible!

I can't talk about clutch performances without mentioning the name Reggie Miller. Do you remember when he stunned the New York Knicks in Madison Square Garden with eight points in the dying seconds of the 1995 Eastern Conference Finals? His Pacers were down six points with 18.7 seconds remaining, when Miller hit a three. He immediately stole the inbounds pass, stepped back behind the arc, and hit another three to tie the game. A few seconds later, he was fouled and knocked down both free throws to close out the Knicks. Wow!

***

These athletes, along with many others, found ways to deliver unbelievable performances under enormous amounts of pressure. The question that always intrigued me was: *How?*

It certainly never felt like there was an element of luck involved. Sure there was some skill needed (to throw a ball, shoot a puck, or shoot a basketball), but these performances must have been the result of having an exceptional mind. A mind that could focus, with composure and confidence.

Some say this ability is natural, but more recently in my coaching career, I have come to the realization that athletes have a great deal of control over their mind. They can train it for big-time situations.

I've played sports for almost forty years, coached for twenty-five, and taught for twenty. During this time, I've heard the words *mental training for performance* more times than I can count. They are buzzwords floating around the sporting community, and yet it seems like so many athletes don't know how to train their mind.

For years, these words continually went in one ear and out the other, remaining somewhat mystical. However, that all changed after an interesting experience in Thailand...

***

For the first thirteen years of my working life, I was a teacher and coach at the University of Winnipeg. I loved my job, but had to start over when my partner Angie and I moved to the West Coast. I was fortunate to be able to stay on part time with the university, teaching month-long courses overseas in the areas of sport and science.

One of the teaching placements was in Bangkok, Thailand. Since the class ran in the evenings, I had loads of time during the day. I needed things to do.

During the flight over, I set some goals for the month over a Thai beer. *Singha,* to be exact. One of my goals was to extend my meditation practice to a full hour. For the past year or so, I had been using the Headspace app and the longest I had meditated for was about twenty minutes. So I had my work cut out for me.

The university set me up in a two-bedroom flat, so I decided to turn the second bedroom into what I soon deemed *the meditation room*. It was completely empty, except for an old rickety wooden chair I placed a short distance from the blank white wall.

On the first day, I put a folded blanket on the seat, to act as a cushion, and buckled down to begin extending my practice. As I began meditating, I heard the intense sounds of Bangkok in the background. I could choose to close the window to diminish the noise, but then the sticky thirty-eight degrees Celsius would soon become a sweltering forty-five. The bulk of the noise was coming from a garage next door, and the rattling sound of changing tires was more than enough to induce frustration in me. After fifteen minutes, I gave up.

After a week of struggle, the following Monday was a Thai holiday. Thankfully, the garage next door was closed. Without the noise, my mind was calmer and more settled. After some time meditating, I opened my eyes to look at the timer and was shocked to see that fifty-five minutes had flown by!

In the last few minutes, I kept my eyes open because the plain white wall that had been in front of me for the past week had turned into a beautiful collage of moving shapes and colours from the sun peeking through the curtains. It was a marvelous moment that I will never forget… maybe because of the beautiful shapes and colours? Possibly because I accomplished my goal? Or both?

When I got up from the chair, I felt like a completely different person. There was a smile plastered on my face that wouldn't go away as I prepared to head out for groceries.

***

The condo building where I was staying, oddly, had a basketball court smack-dab in the middle of the complex. Since I was staying on the far wing, every time I entered or exited the building I had to walk across the court. I had passed by it multiple times since arriving, but this time I decided to put down my backpack, pick up the old, worn-out basketball, and start shooting.

The first handful of shots went in, so I backed up to the three-point line. Shots continued to go in with only a rare miss. I'd played a fair bit of basketball when I was young, but it certainly wasn't my sport. And I hadn't played (or even shot a ball) for years, which made this especially peculiar.

I stopped for a minute, observing that my hands were completely still and not jittery like they usually were at that time of day. Also, my eyes were working better than usual, able to see things in fine detail. And although I had a headache, my concentration was spot-on.

I knocked down a few more shots and, after twenty minutes or so, I left in comical disbelief. As I walked away, I needed to sit down on a nearby bench to process what had just happened. I thought to myself:

I just meditated for an hour and then shot the lights out... What the heck?

Is the state of our mind more important for sport performance than I originally thought?

Did I miss the boat on this one?

Is meditation the key to sport performance?

I left these questions unanswered and carried on to the store.

***

The next day, I was excited to rinse and repeat... another hour of pleasant meditation followed by putting on a shooting clinic. However, the rattling sounds from the garage had returned and I couldn't find the rhythm I'd managed to find the day before. I felt defeated, so decided to pull the chute after about half an hour.

I went down to the basketball court to start shooting, expecting the magic to return, but this time the ball would simply not go in. It hit the front rim, the side rim, the back rim; even an air ball or two was mixed in. The harder I tried, the more it got away from me.

This time, I walked away puzzled. I returned to the same bench to process that day's performance. I thought:

Well, clearly meditation is not the key to sport performance, but could it be the state of our mind?

I left it at that.

***

For the rest of the month, I continued to run my little experiment of meditating, followed by shooting baskets, and then sitting on the bench to reflect. I determined that the state of my mind during meditation was directly correlated with how well I shot the ball. By the end of the month, I could predict how well I would shoot before I even picked up the ball.

This was my aha experience, when I realized that the mind holds the key to unlocking our best performances in sport. Although I'd been told this a thousand times, it wasn't until I experienced it that I began believing it.

***

A seed was planted in Thailand, but that seed needed water, so I spent the next few months down a rabbit hole of googling *mental training for sport*. I was watering the seed in preparation for another season of coaching volleyball.

From my research, I found a variety of mental practices (other than meditation) and tested them out on my tennis game. When I found something

I liked, I put it into a growing collection of tools I planned to use with my athletes in the coming year.

I was entering my second year with this group. Our first season together had been relatively successful on paper, with some good wins down the stretch; however, it was a rocky road. The athletes liked the old way of doing things and questioned my coaching philosophy and tactics.

Going into that second year, I knew big changes had to be made. So my plan was to devote a significant chunk of practice time to the mental side of the game (based on my new hypothesis). It would be a season of training minds, not bodies, and this was the perfect group for it since the school had high academic standards and extra-curricular demands from teachers and parents. My hope was that a change in our state of mind would ease some of the tension and allow us to have a more successful season.

***

In our first mental training session, I had the team do a short meditation followed by writing in their new journals. It felt uncomfortable, especially the idea of sacrificing fifteen minutes of practice time. However, when we went to the gym to practice volleyball, it was by far the best practice we'd had since I started working with this group. It was quieter, with more focus, and the motivation to learn was high.

Before our next practice, I was questioning my new idea. I was tempted to jump ship on the plan until one of the senior players walked up to me and said with an excited tone of voice, "Hey, Mike, can we meditate again today!?" That was enough to give me confidence in the plan and continue moving forward.

We regularly met before practices in our little classroom, meditating, writing, talking, planning. That year I was a teacher, not a coach. Every Monday I would hand out a sheet to each of the athletes consisting of my reflections of the past week, followed by my goals for the upcoming week. After doing this a number of times, one of the athletes said, "I love these!" It was comments like these that added more water to my seed, which had now sprouted.

As the season went on, it became evident that the mental training was working. Everything became clearer for the athletes, who were now buying into my philosophy, which was quickly evolving to focus on the mental side of volleyball. We became a cohesive team, played with consistency, and won with regularity.

In the zone final, we came across a team that hadn't lost all year. Earlier in the tournament, I overheard a coach from another team say, "They're a shoo-in to win it all." It was hard to argue since they were bigger, more athletic, and more experienced than we were.

As the match began, we were tenacious—you could see it in our eyes. We wanted it more, playing some of the best defense I've ever seen at that level.

In the final few points, we were able to shock everyone, including ourselves, with a 15-13 victory.

For the first time in my coaching career, I coached a team that not only met, but exceeded potential in the playoffs. It was one of the most fulfilling coaching experiences I'd ever had, and I'm certain it was because of the time we put into sharpening our minds off the court.

The seed that was planted in Thailand was now a thriving plant.

***

Today, that plant is a tree. I am convinced that mental training has the biggest impact on sport performance, and is underappreciated. I believe that every high-performance athlete, or team, should make it a significant part of their training program. If it isn't yet, this book is a great place to begin training your mind. And if you've already begun, there will certainly be things from this book to add to your regimen.

This book gives you the collection of mental tools that I've put together over the past decade. The tools are delivered through easy-to-read stories of my experiences. Having been given the tools, you will need to practice them, but they will reward you with performing at your peak, when it matters most. This makes the effort you put in so worth it.

Plant your seed, water it, and watch it grow.

PART ONE
FOCUS

"Concentrate all your thoughts upon the work at hand. The sun's rays do not burn until brought to a focus."
—*Alexander Graham Bell*

1

THINK STRATEGICALLY

NO TALKING OR THINKING

You may not recognize the name Andy Puddicombe, but his story is fascinating. In 1994, while in the middle of a sport science degree in England, Andy unexpectedly fled to travel the world to study meditation. His unexpected decision led him on a ten-year journey to India, Myanmar, Thailand, Australia, and Russia. During this time, he became a Buddhist monk and spent four years training with the Moscow State Circus. He later returned home and completed a degree in circus arts. Aside from all these accomplishments, Andy is best known for cofounding the popular meditation app *Headspace*.

With his knowledge of sport science and experience performing in the circus, Andy is an expert in the skill of *focus*. Therefore, we can learn a lot from him on how to perform at our best.

***

Prior to using the Headspace app, I believed that *positive self-talk* was more effective in performance than *negative self-talk*. In other words, if our inner voice is constructive and forward-looking, then performance is enhanced. If our dialogue is down-putting, angry, or aggressive, performance deteriorates.

To this day, I still believe positive talk to be better than negative; however, Andy introduced me to a better alternative:

No talk.

He says, "Talk, of any kind, is not a restful state." This includes positive self-talk because it creates excitement and adrenaline, which we typically don't want in competition.

Andy compares the idea of *no talking* with a predator hunting in the wild. While the predator watches its prey, it is *still*, *quiet*, and *focused*. At the moment before the animal makes its move, there is no positive or negative self-talk. There is no inner voice explaining what to do and no internal speech for motivation. There is simply *total presence of mind*.

***

There are other experts in the field of mental performance that believe talking and thinking hinder performance...

Phil Jackson, who coached his NBA basketball teams to eleven championships, once said, "The secret is not thinking. That doesn't mean being stupid; it means quieting the endless jabbering of thoughts so that your body can do instinctively what it's been trained to do without the mind getting in the way."

Timothy Gallwey, author of *The Inner Game of Tennis*, also advises against thinking. He said, "The greatest efforts in sports come when the mind is as still as a glass lake."

Tennis great Rafael Nadal, who is one of the mentally toughest athletes of all time, says in his autobiography, *Rafa*, "The hardest battle in a match is to quiet the voices in my head, to shut everything out of my mind but the contest itself and concentrate every atom of my being on the point I am playing."

And, finally, D.T. Suzuki said in *Zen in the Art of Archery*, "Man is a thinking reed but his great works are done when he is not calculating or thinking; as soon as we reflect, deliberate, and conceptualize, the original unconsciousness is lost and a thought interferes."

These individuals are masters in the field of mental performance. They seem to be telling us the same thing...

Peak performance stems from a non-thinking mind.

STAY PRESENT

The idea of *no thinking* got me thinking. I thought:

> *In sports that carry on for long periods of time, such as baseball, it seems that it would be nearly impossible to silence our thoughts for the duration of a game.*

> *Not only that, there has to be room for thinking in the form of strategizing, to increase our likelihood of success.*

So my question was:

> *What should ones mind be doing for the duration of a competition?*

***

To answer my question, I called on an expert named Andrei Mandzuk. Andrei is a professor in the sport science department at Douglas College. He is also the founder of *Mzk Performance*, which provides mental performance support for elite athletes. When I met with Andrei, he answered my question well, relating it to a group of high-level golfers he was working with at the time.

Golf is one of the most mentally challenging sports on the planet because of the length of time between shots. This gives the mind many windows of opportunity to take over and destroy a round. This is often done unconsciously.

Pro golfer Phil Mickelson said on *The Ed Mylett Show* podcast, "Things go bad when a player has the inability to control their thoughts." Andrei knows this, so he wanted his golfers to be conscious of their thoughts and steer them toward the present moment.

To do this, Andrei was paying particular attention to the first ten seconds after a shot. His golfers were allowed to let any emotions play out immediately after the shot, at which point they were to direct their focus to cleaning the face of the club. They were to do this with intention, making eye contact with the club while feeling the sensation of touch.

This little action may not seem like much, but it's a crucial moment because it guides the athletes' minds away from reflecting on the outcome of the shot (even though it's only a few seconds old). Andrei said, "There's plenty of time for reflection after a round, when changes can be made before the next one. But making changes within a round is detrimental."

Anyone that's played a fair bit of golf knows how *a tip from a friend* rarely goes in the right direction because adjusting the intricacies of the golf swing causes overthinking. This is why Phil Mickelson said, "I never try to fix the previous swing." Fixing problems may be good during practice, but not during competition, when we want optimal performance.

After cleaning the face of the club, then putting it back in the bag, Andrei's golfers were to remain present, but needed more cues to stay there. So Andrei was asking them to either:

Count their footsteps.

Scan the shape of the treetops.

Note the direction of the breeze.

Another option was to name:

Three things they saw.

Two things they heard.

One thing they felt.

Andrei calls this *broadening the focus.* The goal here was to keep the minds of the golfers busy with things around them. If their minds were occupied in the moment, they couldn't criticize or congratulate themselves on the previous shot. This is in the past. They also couldn't look ahead, toward hoisting any trophies or constructing a list of excuses for a poor round. This is in the future.

As the golfers approach the ball for the next shot, tactical thinking is now allowed, but not until there is a clear observation of the lie. Their thinking should be intentional and strategic for that shot, and only that shot. There should also be no self-talk in the form of motivation such as:

I got this one.

Or negative self-talk such as:

I hate this putt.

Once a plan is made, the athlete can take a deep breath and approach the ball. While standing over the ball, this is when thinking should stop. The mind should become quiet and still —like Timothy Gallwey's glass lake. If a thought interferes, they should back away and again attempt to switch thinking off. Once successful, the focus constricts. Andrei calls this *narrowing the focus.*

Once the shot is performed, Andrei's golfers go back to the beginning of their routine—cleaning the face of the club. Throughout a round, they repeatedly *power down* (broaden) and *power up* (narrow) their focus, always ensuring their minds stay within the constraints of the current moment.

If an athlete attempts to have detailed (or laser) focus for five hours of golf, this is unsustainable from a mental energy standpoint. On the contrary, if they have expansive (or lightbulb) focus for the duration of the round, they won't be able to execute on their shots. Therefore, it's important to alternate between the two.

***

With this in mind, let's revisit Andy Puddicombe's analogy of a predator hunting in the wild. While the animal is looking for prey, it has a broad focus, smelling for scents and watching for rustling in the bushes. When they spot their prey, there's a window of opportunity to think and make a plan. The animal thinks:

> *If this rodent moves behind the rock, I won't*
> *be able to catch him, but if he steps toward*
> *the tree, I can cut him off.*

The predator gets into a hunting stance while their mind goes quiet and their body becomes still. They've narrowed their focus, with a non-thinking mind.

When their prey moves toward the tree, wham-o, lunch is served.

YOUR BREATH IS THE TICKET

On a trip to Whitehorse, I was fortunate to meet Yukon's head squash pro Gyanendra Singh, who goes by the nickname "G." G played professional squash for many years in India, Kuwait, Dubai, and Singapore, and is now an extremely knowledge-able coach. He completed a master's degree in sport science, researching the biomechanics of the drop shot. He is also a practitioner of yoga, specializing in *pranayama*, or breathing.

I was lucky—I timed my trip perfectly for the annual Yukon Open squash tournament. In the finals, G squared off against a younger, less experienced player (but a lethal shot-maker). The match turned into a battle of stamina, both physically and mentally.

Squash is a sport that has intense fitness demands because it's a game of constant agility where there is only a handful of seconds between points for the body and mind to recuperate. G assured me that although this time is brief, it is paramount. He stated:

"Between points, I am sure to never make eye contact with any spectator because it may bring on a thought unrelated to the match. I take a *relaxation breath* to reduce the number of thoughts, then a *power breath* right before I serve. Paying attention to my breath helps me stay focused on my opponent and the current situation. If my opponent shows signs of fatigue and I am aware of it, I'll quickly grab the ball and get ready to serve. If I am the one tired, I'll slow the game down by wiping the sweat off my hand or bounce the ball a few extra times before serving. Many times I've even untied and re-tied my shoe."

G lost the fourth game to even the score at 2-2 as they headed into a fifth and deciding game. He felt like he tried too hard in the fourth game, missing shots that weren't there because he wasn't patient enough.

So to prepare for the fifth game, G went to the bathroom and splashed cold water on his face to regroup. He took a few extra seconds on top of the allotted ninety-second break because he knew that two minutes was the length of time it takes the body to replenish energy stores. These are actions of a true sport scientist. While resting and breathing, his opponent was on the court hitting balls against the wall to himself. These actions require more energy expenditure.

G had the extra burst in the fifth game as he won the match and took home the championship trophy. The difference was his mastery of the mental game, using his breath as a tool.

Meditation legends say that *breath is master of mind*. If you believe that *mind is master of sport*, then:

> *Your breath is the ticket to mastering your sport.*

USE YOUR SENSES

Back in my late twenties and early thirties, I ran four half-marathons and one full. At that time in life, I was blind to the happenings in my mind. So for the purpose of this book I needed to experiment with an endurance sport. Since running long distances was a thing of the past, I decided to do a long bike ride.

I was heading to Duncan (a small city on Vancouver Island) for a meditation course. I figured that pedalling from the ferry terminal in Nanaimo to Duncan would be a challenging distance for someone that only bikes to and from work. The distance is about fifty kilometres, and Google Maps showed it would take me about three and a half hours to complete.

***

I felt great for the first hour, but the ride got more and more challenging as fatigue set in. Cycling long distances, I found, is similar to meditation, except that my eyes were open and my legs were moving. It reminded me of what Phil Mickelson said: "Golf is like a four-to-five-hour meditation session." So in a way, golfers and cyclists meditate as they navigate their way to the finish line.

As I continued to ride, I used my senses to stay present—focusing on:

Sights.

Sounds.

Smells.

Body sensations.

I found that my best cycling was done when I was focused on my breath, which could be categorized under *sensations*. Regardless of what it's categorized under, it's in the present moment, and this helped to control my thoughts. Also, by *stretching* my breath, I felt more relaxed, and this seemed to deliver more oxygen to my muscles. It was also clear that mind-wandering should be avoided at all costs, since my breath became short and shallow during these times. This increased fatigue.

As I neared the end, I continued to focus my attention on breathing fully and completely. Almost five hours later, I arrived in Duncan. Google Maps must not have accounted for the hills. Either that or they thought I had an e-bike?

***

I know one thing is for sure—if I didn't have access to the skills I learned in meditation, there's no way I would have made it to Duncan. I learned from this experience that endurance sports have a large mental component to them because there is ample opportunity for the mind to sail away. This is detrimental to performance. Meditation and breath-work are great tools for long-distance athletes because they improve *focus,* while keeping the body *relaxed* and *energized.*

COUNT

The oldest trick in the books to fall asleep is to count sheep. Why does it work? Because counting is in the present moment, which distracts the mind from thinking about the past or future. This calms the mind.

Counting is used in the Headspace app. Instructions are to count your breaths up to ten while meditating. Once you get to ten, start back at one and repeat. If you are up for a challenge, close your eyes and try counting your breaths up to a hundred. Your goal is to get there without losing track or falling asleep. If you want to achieve expert status, count your breaths to a hundred and then back to one. Counting down is more difficult than up because it requires more concentrated attention. If you make it there and back, well done—you have an outstanding ability to focus.

***

When pro tennis star Novak Djokovic was asked how he avoids succumbing to distractions in clutch moments, he responded with, "I consciously breathe first." Then, as he prepares to serve, he counts his bounces and always ends on an odd number. Many times he will end with nine, eleven, or even thirteen bounces, which is an inordinately high number. The counting keeps him present, while the extra bounces are his time to *out-think* his opponent (or shall we say... *under-think* his opponent).

This is Novak's way of winning the mental war.

***

It's important to note that Novak's strategy of excessively bouncing the ball doesn't work for all tennis players. Yevgeny Kafelnikov, who won two grand-slam titles during his career, routinely bounced the ball only once before serving. If he had employed a strategy of bouncing the ball numerous times, he'd probably psych himself out and miss the majority of his serves. It's possible that Kafelnikov's "one bounce strategy" was his way of *not thinking* about the point. Or maybe he liked to play quickly, which doesn't give his opponent any time to prepare for the return.

Whether a tennis player decides to bounce the ball one time, or thirteen times, the most important thing is to have a strategy. Bounce the ball a set number of times, and count them, because in that moment the mind is fully present.

FOCUS DOESN'T KNOW PRESSURE

The night before a big sporting event, butterflies can be a problem. To deal with this, we've all tried telling ourselves:

I'm not nervous.

Or:

This competition means nothing.

However, it's nearly impossible to convince ourselves of this in a short period of time since our mind knows what's going on and what's at stake.

To deal with pre-game jitters, let's use words of wisdom that Andy Puddicombe gives us on the Headspace app:

Focus doesn't know pressure.

Andy says that pressure comes from the inner dialogue that runs through our head, but this pressure cannot exist in moments when we are intently focused. So the best approach to handling nerves is to continually move our concentration to where we want it—*in the now.*

***

One activity that's increasing in popularity for mind management among athletes is *colouring*. Adult colouring books are more challenging than children's since they require more focused attention to stay in the detailed lines. This provides the benefit of having our mind engaged, distracting it from the upcoming competition.

Not only that, but according to *Beaumont Health*, "Colouring has the ability to relax the fear centre of the brain, the amygdala. It induces the same state as meditating by reducing the thoughts of a restless mind."

While colouring, if you catch your mind wandering toward the upcoming performance, gently move your focus back to the page. The upcoming competition is in the future, so leave it there.

SETTLE THE FISHBOWL

Iryna, a volleyball player I coached many years ago, came to me with a problem. She told me, "I can serve really well in practice but not in a game." Performing better in practice is a common problem for many athletes, and one you've probably encountered at some point in your career.

Since Iryna had success serving in practice, I knew something was getting in her way during games. *Thinking* was most likely the culprit since thoughts arise with more frequency and intensity when pressure rolls around. My hunch told me her thoughts were about the possibility of missing her serve. In other words, she had a *fear of failure*.

As a remedy, I gave Iryna a tip that was shared with me a few years earlier:

> *"Imagine your stomach is a fishbowl filled with water...*
>
> *Make sure the water is completely still before you serve."*

When I told her this, she looked at me with confusion since she was likely expecting some sort of technical advice. Nevertheless, she agreed to try it out.

Midway through our next tournament, Iryna ran up to me in excitement and said, "Hey, that fishbowl thing really works!" It worked because it brought her attention to her stomach, and away from thinking about the outcome of her serve. In other words, she was focusing, which doesn't know pressure.

HAVE A RESET CUE

Neil, a long-time tennis student of mine, would commonly get upset after he made errors. His frustration would compound as a session progressed and he'd end many lessons fuming.

Before a practice one day, I explained to Neil how a *reset cue* is a conscious mental action that can be used to wipe away past mistakes. "If you can continually do this during a session," I told him, "you'll be in a better state of mind toward the end."

I gave Neil a few examples of resets, such as *settling the fishbowl* or *taking a breath*, but I wanted Neil to come up with his own cue. I asked him to keep an eye out for something he wanted to use. He agreed and off we went.

Near the end of the session, Neil was in a better frame of mind. We were playing a few points when I became aware of a tapping sound. It was coming from Neil's racquet touching the ground before every point. I had a hunch this was his reset cue and he later confirmed that indeed it was. Neil told me he loved the concept of deleting the past by performing a small, simple action that required conscious attention.

A few days later, he informed me that he was using this mental tool at work. Reset cues became a handy tool in Neil's mental toolbox.

***

Come up with your own reset cue. Choose something that:

> *You'll remember to do.*
>
> *Is in the present moment.*
>
> *Requires conscious attention.*
>
> *Takes an appropriate length of time.*
>
> *Is a neutral action (not positive or negative).*

MOVE YOUR MIND

Years ago, I was coaching volleyball to a group of seventeen-and-under boys. We travelled to Calgary for a three-day tournament and started off with a long day of volleyball on the first day.

We played well in our opening match, and then had a one-game break where we hung around the gym to watch other teams play.

In our second match, we didn't play particularly well.

Next up was a two-game break. Since we didn't have time to go back to the hotel, the team wanted to stick around the gym and watch more volleyball. I had a bad feeling about this. Hanging around the gym (with continuous whistles blowing and crowds cheering) would only add to the disorder in our heads. So I gathered everyone up and told them we were going outside for a walk. Walking wasn't something on their radar, so they put up a fuss, but I dragged them out the door nonetheless.

It was a beautiful day in May. After a few minutes of walking, they started to cheer up as we stumbled upon a little park. A few guys hit the swings, a couple the teeter-totter, while others threw around a random deflated ball that had been left at the park. Later, a game of tag broke out. It was like the guys were out for recess, turning back the clock ten years and having a blast.

In our next game after the break, there was a renewed sense of energy as we played one of our best matches of the year. Getting outside, where the sun was shining and the birds were chirping, was a big reason for our success because it gave our minds a break.

On Sunday, when I told the guys we had a two-game break, their first response was, "Can we go to the park!?"

In sport, when you get stuck in a rut, move your mind to a different environment. When you come back, you'll have a better disposition.

ACCEPT DISTRACTIONS

While I was competing in the men's doubles final of the Victoria Beach tennis tournament one year, our opponent, Kirby, was lining up a second serve when someone in the crowd cracked a beer. It was supposed to be his moment of quiet so he could focus, but instead his mouth salivated over the thought of a cold beer on a hot day. He stopped his routine and started over, but proceeded to double fault. His focus most likely shifted from *serving*, to *beer*, but never made it back to *serving*.

***

In competition, many say to "block it out" in reference to distractions. However, by attempting to block out an interruption, we are telling ourselves that we don't like that particular stimulus. This results in resistance in the mind.

Instead, let's again follow Andy Puddicombe's lead, who says, "Ground the mind to incorporate everything around you, but at the centre is a place of focus that knows what to do." *Incorporating everything around you* is quite the opposite of *blocking it out*. So when someone in the crowd tries to throw you off your game, just be aware of it. Take it in and embrace it. Then narrow your focus on the task at hand.

FOCUS WITH SPEED

A year later, I felt Kirby's pain. I was preparing to return a serve when a bird flew overhead and let out a *squawk* just as my opponent tossed the ball in the air. It was enough to throw off my concentration as I botched the return.

In this situation, there wasn't much time, but the human brain is quick enough to regain focus almost instantaneously. As the bird flew overhead, I needed to quickly take in the sound, then immediately turn my attention back to the ball (with maximum concentration on the ball). In a split second, my mind should have gone from the *ball*, to the *bird*, then back to the *ball*. Unfortunately I got stuck on *bird*.

***

Train your mind to combat distractions by learning to shift your focus quickly. This is a skill, which can be improved by doing the following:

1. Close your eyes.

2. Use an anchor (such as the breath) to focus your mind.

3. Focus intently on your anchor.

4. When a noise or other distraction comes about, quickly shift your attention to it.

5. Process what the distraction is.

6. Immediately move your attention back to your anchor.

7. Re-focus intently on your anchor.

8. Repeat the above steps and attempt to increase the speed at which you move your focus.

After practicing this for a significant amount of time, you will be able to shift your focus with lightning-quick speed when a bird, or beer, tries to throw you off your game.

USE GUIDANCE-TALK

In sports that are intermittent, like tennis, golf, and squash, it is essential to have a *mental routine* to use between actions. A good mental routine consists of a few words that are to be spoken under an athlete's breath. This is self-talk; however, unlike positive and negative self-talk, these words are spoken in a neutral tone of voice. The words are used to guide thinking, which is why I like to call this type of talk *guidance-talk*.

An example of a mental routine that has worked well for a few of the athletes I've coached is:

>*Breathe.*
>
>*Visualize.*
>
>*Focus.*

Breathe reminds the athlete to take a breath to mentally reset, wiping away the previous point. *Visualize* is then used to imagine the upcoming serve, or return of serve, and exactly where the athlete wants the ball to go. *Focus* is the final cue, geared toward turning our "thinking switch" to off. When this happens, athletes set the stage for performing *out of their mind.*

TAKEAWAYS

- ➤ Positive self-talk is better than negative, but both should be avoided in competition.

- ➤ Immediately before and during play, narrow your focus.

- ➤ Broaden your focus between plays.

- ➤ If you are a long-distance athlete, practice meditation and breath-work to improve your focus, keep you calm, and raise your energy levels.

- ➤ Have access to a reset cue that's used to wipe away the past.

- ➤ If you are nervous before or during a competition, remind yourself that *focus doesn't know pressure.* Continually focus on things in the present moment.

- ➤ Keep your mind busy the night before a competition. Use an activity like colouring.

- ➤ Don't block out distractions. Take them in and accept them for what they are.

- ➤ Learn to shift your focus quickly.

- ➤ Create a mental routine between actions.

- ➤ Use guidance-talk to govern your thinking and actions.

2

CREATE SPACE

DECLUTTER YOUR MIND

Ever since I was a kid, I've spent my summers at our family cottage in Victoria Beach, Manitoba. It's a unique place, situated on a peninsula, where vehicles are prohibited. Cottagers travel by foot and bike, to and from the numerous activities around the beach. One of the major activities is tennis, which is my activity of choice at the beach.

Every August long weekend, the courts host the annual open tennis tournament. It's a tournament that attracts a huge number of competitors; more than any other tournament in Manitoba. The large draws consist of a wide range of ages where it's not uncommon to see a sixteen-year-old playing against a sixty-year-old. The tournament also has a rich history of attracting big crowds; therefore, the diverse cast of competitors are never short of pre-game jitters.

Even though I am one of the more experienced participants in the tournament, I am far from immune to the anxiety that goes hand-in-hand with the tournament. I can remember countless times feeling sick to my stomach before a match. Although I've never turned over my breakfast, it sure has been close, especially when the Saturday night adult dance is combined with an early Sunday morning match.

***

Reflecting back on almost thirty years of competing in this tournament, there is one match I will never forget...

The sun was shining on centre court for the finals, as it seems to do every year on Monday of the August long weekend. My long-time partner Stephen and I were up against a young-gun named Alex, partnered with our long-time rival, Kirby.

Momentum in the match went up and down like a teeter-totter. We won a bunch of games in a row, then lost a bunch in a row, in a sport where alternating games by holding serve is considered good quality. The match was ripe for the picking but nobody wanted it, with most points being terminated by errors, not winners. At one point, it felt like I was trying to hit a golf ball with my tennis racquet.

The match continued to sway back and forth as we found ourselves in a three-hour marathon. It came down to a third set tiebreaker to decide the winner. As I waited for the tiebreaker to start, I had intense feelings of stress. My heart was racing and my breathing was high in the chest—with difficulty getting air in and out.

We started the tiebreaker by trading points back and forth, but again, nobody could step up. The play was poor, even though it was an exciting match for the crowd as it went deep into extra points. As the game tightened, so did the grip on my racquet.

Finally, we had a match point! However, we missed a routine volley, then dumped a forehand return into the bottom of the net, and ended the match with a double fault. It was a devastating defeat to a low-calibre thriller.

***

After the match, I had a deep-down feeling of disappointment. The question of *why did I perform so poorly?* remained unanswered for many years. It wasn't until later in life, when I started to learn about my mind, that I uncovered the reason for the flop…

A few months before the event, I had quit my full-time teaching job. Although it turned out to be the right career move in the end, it caused a great deal of worry in the near term. Leading up to the match, I was constantly thinking about how to make my life work financially. This took up a lot of space in my mind, which negatively affected my ability to perform on the tennis court.

***

Shunryu Suzuki, author of *Zen Mind, Beginner Mind*, said, "It is impossible to organize things if you yourself are not in order." So leading up to a big competition or performance, be sure to get your life in order. Pay all bills, keep your to-do list to a minimum, catch up on emails, do the dishes, and make your bed. Oh, and be sure not to quit your job.

SET THE TABLE FOR EXCELLENCE

Being *in the zone* is something that many professional athletes often talk about, but it's difficult for them to put the feeling into words. Michael Jordan said, "It wasn't me, it was the moment" after draining six straight three-pointers in game one of the 1992 NBA finals. Other athletes say it's "an out of body experience." While some use the word "unconscious."

I felt like I had experienced the zone in a few tennis matches where I played really well. However, it wasn't until a warm summer evening in 2012 that I truly experienced what it felt like to play unconsciously. Here's how it unfolded...

My regular partner, Stephen, was out of town, so I paired up with Alex, who had always been on the other side of the net prior to this tournament. We found ourselves in the final after a good semifinal win. I was the first of the four to arrive for the match so I went straight onto the court. Alex had just finished the singles final and was cramping from the excessive amount of tennis he had played in the thirty Celsius heat. The tournament director came onto the court to inform me that the start time would be delayed another fifteen minutes so Alex could tend to his cramps. I agreed.

Being the only one on the court, and having nothing to do, I closed my eyes. This was a bizarre thing for me to do at the time, since this was well before I had begun meditating and therefore I wasn't aware of the effectiveness of clearing my mind to excel in sport. I took a few deep breaths, felt the heat of the sun on my body, then noticed my beating heart, which was slow and steady. I heard sounds of random banter coming from the crowd, combined with birds chirping, and a few balls being knocked back and forth over on court three. I then imagined a few shots gently coming off the strings of my racquet and landing exactly where I wanted them.

After a few minutes, I woke from my trance as I heard footsteps. I opened my eyes to see Alex hobbling onto the court like he had aged twenty years in a day. We had a minute to talk strategy before our opponents arrived, so I told him I wanted to stand in the middle of the court to take as many shots as possible, since he was somewhat immobile. He agreed.

Early on in the match, I felt calm, with an inner confidence I'd never felt before. Soon, I was firing on all cylinders. Everything that hit my racquet landed exactly where I wanted it, much like I had imagined a short time earlier.

Alex and I won the first set.

In the second set, Alex's cramps started to subside so he told me he was ready to go back to normal formation. At that point, I knew I was in the zone, so I told him, "No way, I'm not changing anything." He reluctantly agreed.

We went on to win the match in straight sets. It was a near-flawless performance.

***

Since that day, I've had some great matches but none of them had that special feeling. The pros were right, it was as if my subconscious mind took over my conscious mind and everything happened naturally. It felt like a blur.

I'd love to be in that empty space again, but it seems like the stars need to be aligned to be back. One of those stars is a few minutes of sitting with eyes closed prior to a competition. It calms the mind, setting the table for excellence.

LOAD YOUR MUSCLES

I had an amazing experience teaching a month-long course for the University of Winnipeg in China. The course was in a city called Zheng Zhou, which is a small city by Chinese standards of roughly thirteen million people. This was my first time in China and I felt the culture shock immediately, especially being a blonde-haired Caucasian male in a city where the number of tourists I met could be counted on one hand.

Despite the initial culture shock, it turned into a great experience. One of my fondest memories was pedalling up and down the streets on an old, beaten-down cruiser-bike with the pungent smell of sewer in the background. Many times I would stop to observe the bustle of the city take place in front of my eyes.

***

The group I taught was a small class of only five students.

On the first weekend, they invited me on a day-trip to the Shaolin Temple, an architectural marvel filled with beautiful artwork, but most famous for being the birthplace of kung fu.

Before the trip, I did some reading about the temple to learn a bit about it. I found a few interesting things…

First, the recruiting process used by the temple to find young martial artists is unique. The Shifus (which I learned is the term for a kung fu master) go into city schools and hand-pick the young children that seem to be the right fit for Shaolin. These are the students that are generally uninterested in school-work and have some athletic qualities.

Second is the training. When the youngsters first arrive at the temple, the first step they undertake is to train their mind. The Shifus of the Shaolin Temple understand that a strong mind is essential for kung fu, which is why they institute training for it on day one. Once the youngsters get to a good point mentally, stage two is to develop the athletic abilities, such as flexibility, balance, agility, and strength, and sort of in that order. Finally, not until stage three do the artists begin the flashy kicks and punches that you see in the movies.

The reading I did was compelling, since the three-stage training plan of the Shaolin Temple was the opposite of what we do here in North America. We typically start with the sport, playing games and competing right away. Then, as we get older, we start to develop athletic abilities. Not until later in life do we start to understand the importance of the mind and possibly begin to train it.

In much of the Eastern world, the importance of the mind has been understood for centuries. In the west, it's now catching on, mainly because athletes and coaches are now realizing that mental training truly works.

***

At the temple, there are performances put on every few hours. After waiting in line for over an hour, the students and I were finally able to get in. It turned out to be well worth the wait since the displays of athleticism from artists of a variety of ages were mind-blowing. Each artist had an amazing ability to move—with speed, agility, and grace—like cats. They were also extremely focused. This could be seen in their eyes.

The final performance was particularly interesting. It was done by one of the older, more experienced martial artists. He had a loftier goal than the others: to kick through what looked to be about ten pieces of wood (about half-an-inch thick each). He approached the challenge in front of him with a slow and composed walk, then closed his eyes for about twenty seconds as a hush went over the crowd. Then, with an explosion of incredible force, he struck through each and every piece of wood. I looked down the aisle at our group, and they looked back at me with a similar facial expression—one that said, *Wow!*

***

After the performance, the martial artists hung around the concourse thanking everyone for coming with little more than a bow of their head. They were grounded, with stoic facial expressions that meant nothing but business.

Off to the side was an older gentleman that looked like a Shifu, and when he saw me, he belted out *Hello!* in broken English. He had spent time in the United States and was excited to speak English with me, and share his knowledge and experience at the temple.

In the conversation, I asked him why the final performer closed his eyes prior to striking his target. He told me the artists were trained from a young age in *Qigong*, which is a popular Chinese practice of:

Meditation.

Breathing.

Movement.

The training in Qigong allowed the older performer to use his breath, which not only placed him in the moment, but was used to *load his muscles*. The Shifu said that we often keep our breath high in the chest, and not down in the diaphragm, so it's imperative to take a few long exhales to release all the air in the lungs.

This is what the performer did during the twenty seconds. He worked toward bringing his breath deep into his diaphragm. This enabled him to take in a big gulp of oxygen immediately before the strike, then let it all out on contact. He did this by letting out a roar.

***

I thought long and hard on the bus ride home about my experience at the temple. I first learned that it's never too early to start training the mind. I wondered how my sporting life would have been different if I had been subjected to the same training program as the young artists at Shaolin.

I also learned the importance of using the breath prior to a sporting action that requires force. It not only helps with focus, but by deepening the exhale, we create space in the muscles. This translates into more force.

TAKE A MAGIC MINUTE

Laird Hamilton is a retired big wave surfer who preaches the importance of the mind in his sport. Surfers deal with the potential of death every time they catch a behemoth wave. A friend of mine told me about a quote he had heard from Laird:

> *"You don't need to warm up the body;*
> *however, you need to be mentally ready."*

I decided to experiment with this before going for a workout. Instead of doing my regular movement patterns and dynamic stretches, I sat on an exercise ball, closed my eyes, and attempted to prepare my mind. I took a few breaths and set an intention for the day. My intention was:

> *To be efficient.*
>
> *To breathe deeply.*
>
> *To not care.*

Efficiency meant I wanted to be in and out of the gym in forty-five minutes, but still pump out a quality workout. In order to do that, I would spend very little time resting between sets while moving quickly from exercise to exercise.

Breathe deeply meant I wanted full inhales and exhales to not only lift more weight, but breathing would be my cue to stay on task.

Lastly, I didn't want to *care* about what others thought of me, particularly the guy that was three times my size who always poked fun at how little weight I had on the bar. Although he spoke in a somewhat joking tone of voice, it found a way to irritate me. On this day, I wanted to simply acknowledge his comments and carry on with my workout.

I opened my eyes and got right to work. Sure enough, forty-five minutes later, I walked out the door with a quality workout under my belt. And I was so efficient that the big dude didn't get a chance to come over and mock me. Most workouts take me a few hours to get the same amount of work done, getting distracted by the sports on the TVs or chatting with others. On other days, I don't even finish the workout, or put in very little effort because I am either *too stiff*, *too tired*, or *too injured*. However, these obstacles can be overcome by using the breath to settle down and set an intention. It only takes a minute and is pretty magical.

***

Take a *magic minute* to mentally prepare for a competition by doing the following:

1. Stand up straight (hold hands in a circle if you are on a team).

2. Close your eyes.

3. Take five *relief breaths* where you breathe in through the nose and let the breath fall out the mouth.

4. Take five *relaxation breaths* where you breath in slowly through the nose, then breath out long and fully through the nose.

5. Feel energy in the hands.

6. Feel energy in the feet.

7. Set your intention for the day.

8. Open your eyes.

9. Take five *power breaths* where you breathe in through the nose and out through the mouth (short and fast).

If possible, this exercise should be done at the location where you will be competing. This allows you to become more familiar with the sounds, smells, and overall feel of the environment. It gives your unconscious mind a feeling that everything is OK and that you are safe, since your fight-or-flight response is certain to be active before the big show.

This exercise should only take a minute, maybe two, but certainly no more than three. If you overdo it, you'll feel half-asleep, and not *alert, attentive,* and *ready.* For many athletes, more than a minute or two of relaxation is needed to bring the stress response down. If that's the case, do a longer relaxation session well before the competition to stabilize your mind. Then introduce movement to get all the systems firing. A few minutes before go-time, sneak in a magic minute to recall the relaxation response you tapped into earlier in the day. You will feel poised and ready to perform. I promise.

BODY, BREATH, AND MIND

Living in Kitsilano, a neighborhood in Vancouver, I adhere to the yoga lifestyle by walking or biking around town with a yoga mat and healthy greens strapped to my back. Before a yoga class, taking a magic minute is common practice and I always look forward to this time. My mind is often in fast-forward when I arrive at a class, so lying down, taking a few deep breaths, and setting an intention seems to free up some space. When the class commences, my ability to perform the poses and postures is more effective than if I had gone straight into the class. The magic minute puts my train on the right track.

***

During one particular yoga class, the instructor made a few references to "finding space." I spoke with her after the class since I was writing about *space* in this chapter. She said that yoga creates space in three areas:

→ First, we create space in the *joints* by performing static poses and dynamic movements. This increases our flexibility and range of motion.

→ Second, we create space in the *lungs*, *diaphragm*, and *chest* with proper breathing.

→ And third, we create space in the *mind* by staying present.

The instructor concluded with, "By focusing on these three areas, we are sure to have a great class and feel amazing afterward."

***

When I got home, I thought about the conversation I had with the yoga instructor and the link between yoga and sport. *Body*, *breath*, and *mind* are deeply connected, and when we free-up space in all three, we lay the foundation for a wonderful performance.

GET ALL YOUR DUCKS IN A ROW

While teaching at the University of Winnipeg in the Faculty of Kinesiology, I did a lesson on the importance of *preparation*. A week or so later, a student came up to me after class and explained how the lesson helped him immensely with the poorly behaved children he had been teaching to ski. He told me he had spent extra time preparing for his last session and it had gone really smoothly.

I found this particularly interesting since this student was certainly old enough to know the importance of being well prepared, but it wasn't until the word was put front-and-centre in his brain that it became a priority. Instead of expending mental energy worrying about the behaviour of his group, he spent that time planning a detailed practice. Afterwards, he had a feeling of pride and accomplishment because his vision of a perfect practice became a reality.

***

Abe Lincoln said:

> *"If you give me four hours to chop down a tree, I'll spend the first three sharpening the axe."*

So prepare for an important competition by making a detailed agenda of what you will do for the twenty-four hours building up to the start time. This is your *mental preparation plan*, which ensures that your mind is as sharp as Abe's axe.

THE SPACE BETWEEN

In meditation, there's a concept known as *the space between*. It comes between breaths. When air is actively moving in and out of the nose, there is movement in the stomach and chest, combined with the sound of the inhale or exhale. But when you pause to reverse the flow, there is a still, quiet moment that can be of value.

After reading about the space between breaths, I decided to try it out at home. Sure enough, there were short segments of time that were calm and quiet. I found it interesting that this led to a very focused and peaceful session. This is because I was always present, either in the space, or anticipating the space.

I sat down a few days later, excited to find more space. However, the sounds of construction outside my window made it very challenging. Although I couldn't find my breath over the noise, I was able to find some space when the harsh sounds momentarily stopped. As time went on, I used the intermittent noise to my advantage by appreciating the times when it wasn't there. After a choppy start to the session, it surprisingly ended well.

**

I thought about the concept of space and its connection with sport. I figured:

> *If the space between breaths is important to*
> *find stillness in a meditation session, then*
> *the space between actions is important while*
> *competing in sport.*

I also thought:

> *On some days, it's noisy, but by finding*
> *some space early on, an athlete can gather*
> *themselves and put together a decent day.*

**

Although volleyball can be a rowdy sport, I found a nice, quiet moment before every point. When the referee blows the whistle to commence play, the crowd quiets down while the server bounces the ball a few times. Then, just before the server tosses the ball up, there is silence while they hold the ball in their hand.

Once I discovered this, I directed my athletes to find this space, and to simply be aware of the silence in this moment. If they could find space before every serve through the course of a match, it had the potential to keep their minds in a better place. This is easy to do, but the trick is to remember to do it.

***

Since a non-thinking mind is the key to sporting excellence, we need ways to turn our brain off. *Finding space* is one way. At the highest level of many sports, the contest is won or lost during the space between. In golf, there is a lot of space. In volleyball, there is very little. Regardless, this time is so valuable.

While you compete, look for quiet moments. Be fully present at these times and enjoy the silence. If you can repeatedly locate space, it leads to a peaceful disposition throughout the competition. And a peaceful disposition is the frame of mind associated with *the zone*, which is where sporting masterpieces are created.

MENTAL GATHERING

Many sports have designated spaces within a competition. They can come in the form of a time-out, intermission, half-time, etc. In volleyball, for example, teams are allowed two sixty-second time-outs per set, plus a three-minute break between sets.

I spent some time thinking about our team's time-outs and whether I was using the time effectively. I quickly realized that, from a mental performance perspective, they were completely inefficient.

My first mistake was giving too many technical instructions, such as:

Keep your elbow high.

Get around the ball.

End on your left foot.

When an athlete is given this type of feedback in a game setting, an error is destined to ensue when they try to make the change. Technique should be taught during practice, when the athlete can have repetitions to try out the new idea and feel more comfortable making mistakes. However, in a game, there is simply too much happening. A better approach to technical changes is to make a list of *things to work on* and explore them in the next practice. Games are for strategic advice.

On top of technical advice, I was also spending time trying to motivate my athletes. At times, motivation is beneficial; however, constant *wanting* and *forcing* created a push-back that stirred up the minds of my athletes (and mine, for that matter). Athletes would come into time-outs wound-up from the competition, and I was winding them up even more.

My competitiveness was working against me, so I needed to step back and relax in order to get more from them.

***

After my reflection, I decided to do a total revamp of our time-outs that season…

The first change was simple. I had the athletes sit down as soon as they came off the court. This is common practice in sports like basketball because there is more of a cardiovascular requirement and athletes need to catch their breath. In volleyball, however, teams commonly huddle standing up. Even though my athletes weren't out of breath from sprinting up and down the court, they needed to sit down to rest their bodies and regroup mentally.

After sitting, I would then remind the athletes to replace fluids—an oft-forgotten aspect in taking care of mind and body.

Next, I had them close their eyes and take a deep breath. I found the best breath to use in this situation is called a *pursed lip breath,* where you inhale through the nose and allow the air to come out of the mouth like you are holding a straw between your lips. Having tight lips forces the exhale to be done slowly, which calms the nervous system.

When the athletes opened their eyes, I finished the time-out with a question, such as:

How are we doing?

Do we need to make any changes out there?

Who's in the front row?

How can we stop number eight?

It's important that the question induced a short discussion around what needed to be done on the very next point. By asking a question about the upcoming point, versus making an evaluation of the past or a hope for the future, this ensured the players there was no judgement from me. Judgement, from anyone, only adds to the mental struggle of competition.

Asking questions also gets athletes more entwined in the decision-making process. This slowly leads to empowerment, where leaders have the opportunity to step forward.

After a few weeks of questioning, the athletes started to run the time-outs themselves. Although I still needed to facilitate, it was nice that they stopped looking to me for the answer every time we experienced some volatility. They had to look within in order to solve problems as a group.

***

Our total time-out makeover was an essential change on our journey toward success. At first, it felt funny for the athletes to close their eyes and take a breath in the midst of battle, but after a while, it became second nature. In fact, many athletes looked forward to time-outs in order to create some space. It's a good time to think, make a plan, and move forward.

This process is called *mental gathering*. When it's done properly, athletes go back to performing with a calmer demeanour and a renewed sense of direction.

UNWIND YOUR MIND

If you've ever met a Vizsla, you'll know that this breed of dog is particularly high strung. Their minds are like one of those little wind-up toys—you know, the ones you get at the dollar store that have a little crank at the back? And when you turn it enough times, then let go, the toy goes haywire?

When Rudy, our Vizsla, was a puppy, I would take him to the dog park to play with other dogs. Within a few minutes of being off-leash, he would often become wound up with excitement or fear. But if I could grab him by the collar and have him sit for thirty seconds or so, he would go back to playing calmer and more under control. This is Rudy's magic minute. Unfortunately, I could never get him to close his eyes and take a deep breath. We're still working on that.

***

Sometimes we may find our mind to be like Rudy's while competing in sport. Before the game even starts, our wind-up toy is cranked up. When the competition begins, this only adds more cranks.

Iconic meditation teacher Satya Narayana Goenka said, "The breath is strongly related to the mind." So take a moment to slow down your breath. It calms your system, releasing the tension in your toy.

TAKEAWAYS

➤ Before a competition, create space in your mind by getting your life in order.

➤ Before performing a sporting action that requires force, load your muscles by deepening your breath.

➤ Take a magic minute within an hour of competition. Use your breath to ground your mind and set an intention for the day.

➤ Create space in the joints, lungs, and mind with movement, breathing, and focus.

➤ Prepare for a competition by making a detailed agenda leading up to the start time.

➤ Look for quiet space. Be aware in these moments and enjoy the silence.

➤ During time-outs and intermissions, consider mental gathering by adding a breath and contemplating your next course of action.

➤ If you find yourself getting wound up before or during a competition, slow your breath to release tension.

3

ENHANCE YOUR FOCUS

LIVIN' IN THE MOMENT

One summer night in Manitoba, I went out with a few friends for a drink. The topic of conversation found its way toward meditation. Alex, a long-time tennis buddy, and his friend Lindsay had both completed a Vipassana course. Vipassana is ten days of meditation, practicing ten and a half hours a day under a vow of silence. The practice of Vipassana is based on the same teachings that were discovered centuries ago by the Buddha.

Alex and Lindsay were excited about doing another ten-day course. This seemed insane to me at the time—that anyone would be *excited* to meditate for ten days straight without being able to talk. They were planning to attend a course in Merritt, BC. Alex asked if he could stay with me before and after the course, since he was flying in and out of Vancouver. I told him that wouldn't be a problem, but when he asked if I wanted to join them on the course, I said, *no way*.

As the conversation went on, they both raved about the benefits they'd experienced following their last course. Alex said it dramatically improved his performance on the tennis court and credited a close three-set victory in the Victoria Beach tournament to the skills he attained in Vipassana. He then rattled on about the benefits Vipassana provided him in his coaching. That was when I really started to listen, since coaching is my main passion.

Prior to that night, I had heard of three famous people that regularly practice Vipassana: Jack Dorsey, Tim Ferris, and Yuval Noah Harari. Jack Dorsey, the former CEO of Twitter, did a ten-day course to "celebrate" his birthday. Tim Ferris, best known for his book *The 4-Hour Work Week*, claims that his first Vipassana course was the turning point in his life. Yuval Noah Harari, best known for writing *Sapiens*, spends a full month every year, and two hours every day, practicing Vipassana. All three had life-changing experiences, along with thousands of others. So the benefits of Vipassana seemed very real.

By the end of the night (with the help of a few glasses of red wine), I agreed to join Alex and Lindsay on the retreat.

***

The first three days of the course were dedicated solely to improving focus. This was done using a technique called *Anapana*, which means *mindfulness of breathing*.

Day one started us off with a general awareness of the breath, attempting to determine which nostril the air was moving through—the left, the right, or both. Early on in the day, staying focused on the breath was difficult since my monkey mind was swinging from branch to branch from a flooding of random thoughts. I also had FOMO (fear of missing out) on all the fun things I could be doing at home.

To make matters worse, that night, it became evident that I was rooming with a snoring machine. He cut down timber the entire night and I got little to no sleep. At one point, I went to the opposite end of the mediation hall and lay down on the carpet, attempting to get a little bit of shut-eye, but I could still hear the faint sound of snoring!

All in all, day one was a struggle.

Day two's instructions were to narrow the focus to sensations in and around the nose and mouth area. If my mind wandered off, I was to simply recognize this and come back to sensations in that area. On this day, I started to get into a better rhythm as thoughts were running their course. My monkey mind was becoming tamer.

The course tightened the focus even more on day three, toward sensations in the small area below the nostrils and above the upper lip—the moustache. By now, I was starting to adapt to the idea of no talking and the extensive amount of meditation. I remembered what Alex said before the course started: "Meditating becomes just what you do. It's like a regular workday. Get up, have coffee, get to work."

By the end of the third day, my mind was as sharp as a knife. At this point, I was able to sense that the air coming into my nostrils was cool and the air going out was warm. In order to feel this temperature difference, the mind needs to be laser-focused. Three days of hard work got me to that point.

On days four through ten, Anapana switches to Vipassana, where we were to scan the body up and down while focusing on sensations. Although we didn't use the breath during Vipassana, focus continued to improve.

As I went deeper, my mind started recalling vivid memories of my childhood. S.N. Goenka, who initiated the intensive ten-day Vipassana course, said, "These ten days are a deep surgical operation of your mind, and when you cut open the wound, puss starts coming up on the surface. It isn't pleasant, but face it bravely since it's for your own good." There certainly was some pain during my surgery, which manifested itself in my lower back. But although there was pain, I found the introspection to be quite fascinating.

On the last day of the course, I limped my way to the finish line. As I lay in bed that night, with my roommate still snoring, I had a similar feeling to running a full marathon in my early thirties.

However, instead of my legs being burnt, it was my brain that felt like a roasted marshmallow.

On day eleven, they let us loose.

***

The first conversation I had was with Alex. It felt strange to talk again but I was excited to share ten days' worth of ideas and insight. It was interesting that listening seemed easier in that conversation. I was able to process information immediately as it came out of Alex's mouth, without any lag. My brain was working quickly, like a rabbit, whereas, prior to the retreat, it lumbered like an elephant.

As I conversed with Alex, I noticed that his eye colour was red. I said to him, "What the heck, your eyes turned red during the course."

He laughed and replied with, "They've always been like that, you just haven't noticed them before."

I scrunched my eyebrows in confusion, wondering how I'd never noticed that he had red eyes after all these years. It was becoming clear that some changes had occurred in me. One change was an ability to see things that I hadn't noticed before.

***

As Alex, Lindsay, and I drove home through the mountains, the feelings of joy I had in the middle of the retreat returned. This time, however, it was pure ecstasy. A few times, I thought I accidentally consumed a really good drug. I had a permanent smile from ear to ear for the entire four-hour drive. It was a deep feeling of happiness that I hadn't felt since I was a kid. The blue sky and snow-covered mountain tops were majestic as Mumford and Sons played on the radio. And the beats moved through my body like pulsating waves.

We stopped at Starbucks and I ordered my usual drip coffee with a shot of cream, but this time it smelled amazing and tasted like heaven.

The conversation with Alex and Lindsay on the rest of the way home was entertaining as we compared and laughed about our experiences during the course. We were *livin' in the moment,* as they say, not questioning the past or worrying about the future.

***

The next day, I had a number of things to take care of to get my life back on track. One task was to change a flat tire that Angie had snagged while I was away. I took the tire off and carried it half a kilometre down the road to get repaired, trudging through an unusual Vancouver snowstorm. This is a task that would usually cause me to curse my way to the garage in anger and frustration, but not this time… I actually enjoyed it! I said *hello* to strangers while we laughed about my awkwardness in lugging a tire over slippery sidewalks.

***

A few days later, I lined up a tennis game with Angus, who was my main hitting partner for the past few years. For the most part, we were evenly matched, but more times than not I would end up on the losing end. He had more experience in singles, combined with some sort of mental edge that I couldn't put my finger on.

When I got to the courts, Angus asked if I had been playing much lately. I told him that I'd just finished a ten-day meditation course.

"What?" he replied. "Ten days of meditation... Holy crap... How do you feel?"

"I feel amazing," I replied. "I've never been so happy even though I have an aching back and am exhausted from practically no sleep."

After a few hits in the warm-up, the first thing I noticed was my new and improved vision. I was able to see the fuzz on the ball as it came toward my racquet. And when the ball made contact with my strings, I was more attuned to the sound. Everything I did, including walking over to pick up the ball, I did with precise focus, pinpointing the most minute details with my senses. But although I had a keen sense of focus, my legs were slow—like my feet were cemented into the ground.

Once the match began, Angus jumped out to a 3-0 lead before I could blink an eye. However, in the fourth game, my legs started to warm up to the idea of movement. I won that game and proceeded to win the next five in a row, an unthinkable string of games for me as I took the first set.

In the second set, I maintained focus while Angus got frustrated. I won that set 6-1. Feeling like the last hour was a blur, I said to Angus as we walked off the court, "What just happened?"

Angus replied, "Good job, man. I got rattled and you clearly had a game plan that you executed on." I smiled, thinking to myself that I hadn't made any plan at all, except to make it through the match without permanently damaging my back and getting carried off on a stretcher.

I went home and did an hour of meditation that evening, trying to continue the Vipassana recommendation of an hour in the morning and an hour in the evening. As I attempted to meditate, my mind wanted to reflect on the stellar performance. I asked myself...

How is this possible?

How could I play so well after sitting on my ass for ten days?

Upon further reflection, I realized that I'd never looked back, or gotten ahead of myself. I'd simply focused on the current point, and done it with precision. On top of that, I was able to maintain focus for over an hour because my mental endurance had been improved during the meditation course.

To put it simply… I could focus, with precision, for an extended period of time. Now, I was able to put my finger on why Angus had a mental edge.

***

In *Zen Mind, Beginner Mind,* Shunryu Suzuki said, "Zen is being total in what you do, giving it your complete attention." When we give *complete attention* to our sport, we achieve greatness. Attention is trained in meditation. So if this ancient practice isn't currently a part of your training program, be sure to layer it in.

Many athletes have gotten to the next level in their sport by making meditation a piece of their training. Some examples are Stephen Curry, LeBron James, Russell Wilson, Novak Djokovic, Phil Mickelson, and Derek Jeter. Outside of sport, famous people that meditate include Oprah Winfrey, Jerry Seinfeld, Bill Gates, Steve Jobs, Joe Rogan, Katy Perry, George Lukas, Will Smith, and Jennifer Lopez. You'd be hard-pressed to come up with a list of more successful people than that!

GET OVER THE HUMP

Three years before I completed my first Vipassana course, I had moved from Winnipeg to Vancouver. It was exciting, but there was a lot of struggle that went along with it. A large part of the challenge came from leaving my teaching job.

With nothing lined up in Vancouver, the first thing I did was frantically look for work. Before I knew it, I'd amassed seven different jobs and was working my butt off to make ends meet.

One of the seven jobs I'd accumulated was teaching private tennis lessons at the local courts. The first person to find my advertisement on Craigslist was Neil, who would become a regular for the next four years.

Neil was a savvy businessman from the UK who carried a competitive nature from playing many years of high-level cricket. He had a strong desire to improve and wanted to practice every day at seven o'clock in the morning before work.

When we had some time after a session, we would sit on the side of the court and chat about life. Sometimes the conversation would get pretty deep.

One day, he was excited about his discovery of the Headspace app. The app is very popular now, but was relatively unknown at the time. Neil raved about the benefits he'd gained over a relatively short period of time and wanted me to try it out. He explained that the app had ten free meditations that should be done over a ten-day span. The word *free* caught my attention, but the word *meditation* was terrifying at that point in life.

I said, "Oh, no! Not for me."

But Neil (with his business background) had a way with words and proceeded to break me down. He said, "You know that you often ask me to do things that take me out of my comfort zone on the tennis court?"

"Yes," I replied.

"Well, it would be a lot more comfortable for me not to try them... to remain as is. But I know that if I don't try them, I won't get any better. Do you agree?"

"Yes," I again replied, sensing where this was going.

"Do you not think this is a similar situation?" Neil responded.

"It is," I said with my head down to avoid eye contact.

"Then I'm asking you to take yourself out of your comfort zone and do one ten-minute meditation every day for the next ten days," said Neil in a firm tone of voice.

I told you he had a way with words, as he managed to convince me to attempt meditation in less than a minute. So I went home, made myself a coffee while downloading the app, then sat in meditation for the first time.

After the ten minutes were up, I wouldn't say I felt any better, but the act of closing my eyes to observe what was going on inside my head had been intriguing. For that reason, and to stick to my promise with Neil, I finished the remaining nine days.

After ten days, I learned that my stress response was much more active than I had originally thought. Especially since I was juggling seven jobs. A hundred minutes of staring at the back of my eyelids was enough to calm down my overactive mind. Neil was the catalyst, pushing me over the edge into trying something that was well out of my comfort zone. Now, I am grateful that he gave me a push because it has helped me in all facets of life.

STAY OVER THE HUMP

Once I was over the hump, I needed a way to stay over the hump, so I continued combining meditation with a cup of coffee in the morning. The coffee sat on my lap as I enjoyed the smell, taking a sip every so often to enjoy the taste. I had drunk coffee for many years prior to trying meditation, but rarely took the time to enjoy it since I was either on the go or my mind was elsewhere. While meditating, however, I could focus on and savour each sip.

Over time, combining coffee and meditation became a part of my routine. To this day, simply smelling the aroma of coffee beans slows down my breath and relaxes my muscles. And every time I sit down to meditate, I salivate, regardless of whether or not there is a cup of coffee on my lap.

Combining coffee and meditation would sound outrageous to the meditation gurus; however, it works for me. For that reason, I carry on.

I told my strange habit to a fellow after finishing a three-day meditation course and he replied with "You can't meditate with coffee on your lap!"

My response was, "Says who? If it helps to motivate me, then why not? Besides, smell and taste are sensations in the present moment. And also, I can use a sip to reset my mind when it drifts off."

***

It turns out I'm not the only one to combine these two activities. Singer-songwriter Leonard Cohen was an avid meditator and needed coffee to stay awake at five o'clock in the morning while meditating with the monks.

So if you are struggling to meditate, try having a cup of java while you close your eyes. Or use another form of motivation to keep you over the hump. Maybe that motivation is to get to the next level of your sport. This will keep you coming back for more.

ONE BREATH, ONE MIND

I grew up watching the Chicago Bulls during their epic run in the nineties. At the time, I appreciated Michael Jordan, Scottie Pippen, and the other stars, but knew very little about Phil Jackson. It wasn't until I read his book, *Eleven Rings*, that I discovered he was a pioneer in training the mind for sport. He understood that *meditation*, *mindfulness*, and *breathing* are powerful tools that can be used in competition.

In his book, Phil explained how mental training became a big part of his coaching. It began at a young age when he had a tough time buying into the strict religious practices pushed onto him by his parents. As a result, he started investigating different cultures.

He learned about Zen Buddhism, Taoism, and the traditional North American Indigenous way of life. He took bits and pieces from each and blended them into his own approach to life and subsequent philosophy of coaching.

As an NBA coach, he was disappointed with the focus of his players in team meetings, claiming they would fidget, with poor eye contact, while he spoke. He also found that many of his athletes struggled in the postseason because they lacked the mental toughness in key moments. So he taught them techniques to improve their ability to concentrate.

Prior to games, the Bulls would sit in a circle with the lights out, breathing and meditating. Phil called this their *circle of life*. The circle symbolized their joining together and bonding as one. While holding hands, he spoke about solidarity, which is a powerful way to change the mindset of his athletes from individualism to unity.

With the Lakers, Phil introduced a concept of *one breath, one mind,* where the team worked together to synchronize their breaths. The breathing exercise not only improved their attention, but symbolized the concept of working together to achieve a goal. This improved the Lakers' chemistry, which was desperately needed prior to Phil's arrival.

Although these types of mental practices are more common in sport nowadays, incorporating them into the NBA was unheard at that time. The basketball community questioned Phil's integration of spirituality into sport. They also questioned other "out-there" practices of Phil's, such as turning the lights out, or not allowing verbal communication during drills. This forced the athletes to use their senses to play basketball.

Although many questioned Phil's tactics, few can argue with his results, highlighted by an unbelievable eleven championship rings in twenty years of coaching. Many people downplay his success, stating he always coached teams with big stars. However, he had a knack for taming egos and creating the team dynamic necessary to win championships. This was done by training the minds of his athletes.

Longtime Laker Kobe Bryant said in an interview, "After coming off six championships with the Bulls, Phil came to our team and had us sit in the film room with the lights out to meditate. Our team started to play with more poise and pressure situations had little effect on us."

In the Netflix docuseries *The Last Dance*, Jordan said (in reference to their championship finals win over the Utah Jazz), "That's where the craftsmanship came in. Ninety-eight was much better than any other year because I was able to use my mind as well as my body."

Phil himself said, "To excel, you need to act with a clear mind and be totally focused on what everyone on the floor is doing. All of us have flashes of greatness... when we're completely immersed in the moment."

These three sporting icons are telling us that a strong mind is imperative for competing in sport, so we should listen. Their words are:

Tame your mind.

BREATHE LIKE A LION

When you think of an image of Michael Jordan, there's a good chance he has his tongue hanging out while dribbling the ball down the court or dunking a basketball. This was one of his trademarks. He says it originally came from watching his dad at a young age stick out his tongue while working on the family car.

Sticking our tongue out is a sign of concentration that tends to happen *naturally* in some. It can often be seen in children when they draw, colour, or cut out paper. Similarly, when we *intentionally* stick out our tongue, we are present in that moment and are able to focus. Not only that, it relaxes the jaw. When we're under stress, the muscles responsible for opening and closing our jaw tighten from unconsciously clenching our teeth. Sticking out our tongue stretches these muscles to relieve some of the tension.

Yogis have understood this for centuries, so encourage a practice called *lion's breath,* where you:

1. Inhale through the nose.

2. Open your mouth wide while sticking your tongue out.

3. Exhale out the mouth, making a "haa" sound as if you are breathing out hot air.

4. Do this thirty or forty times in a row.

Once your breath returns to normal, you should notice a relaxation effect in your body. Use this tool to ease tension a few hours before a competition. Or *be like Mike* and do it during.

READ A BOOK

We can enhance our ability to concentrate not only through meditation but during every waking minute of the day. Instead of doing tasks and activities on auto-pilot, bring your full attention to them. This is *mindfulness*.

While you read this book, for example, you are practicing mindfulness by staying present with the words and their meaning. When your mind floats away (as it inevitably will from time to time), gently bring your attention back to the book.

Phil Jackson understood the value of reading as a mindfulness tool, so would give each of his athletes a book to read. He carefully chose books for the needs of each athlete. Later in the year, he would set up individual meetings with each athlete to talk about the theme of their book and its connection with basketball. The purpose of this activity was to not only teach them a life lesson, but to give them a tool for concentration—which they carried onto the court.

EXTEND YOUR FOCUS

Ayrton Senna was one of the greatest Formula 1 drivers to ever get behind the wheel. At a young age, he found a passion for karting. His mother explains in the documentary *Senna* how Ayrton would sit at the front of his class, listen intently to his teacher, and complete all of his work during class-time so he could have more time in the evenings for karting.

Ayrton was always present, spending the entire school day in focus, and then continuing to concentrate when he got behind the wheel in the evening. Whether he knew it or not, he was training his mind to concentrate for extended periods of time. Mindfulness became Ayrton's most lethal weapon later in life as he amassed forty-one Grand Prix and three world championships.

***

Some sports, such as auto racing, require intense focus for extended periods of time. There is little to no opportunity for broadening the focus in a race that lasts over two hours. If this is a characteristic of your sport, you'll want to train your mind to focus intently for the duration.

It would be difficult to meditate for over an hour if you weren't experienced, but if you had that ability, you'd be the heavy favourite. There are other activities that can be done to improve your focus for longer periods of time, such as watching a movie. Even though it's not as effective as meditation because the environment isn't as controlled, it helps to teach the eyes and ears to stay more attuned.

When it comes time for you to get behind the wheel, you are focused in the moment because you trained that skill by watching movies. While you are dialed in, your opponent is already imagining themselves drinking champagne on the podium. This is your leg up on the competition. And soon, you are the one tilting back the bubbly.

DO ONE THING AT A TIME

Eckhart Tolle, German philosopher and author of *The Power of Now*, says, "Zen is doing one thing at a time."

To expand on Tolle's statement, human consciousness has the ability to quickly switch from one stimulus to another, but it cannot multitask at any one instant. For example, if you put on a podcast before going for a run, you can switch your attention back and forth between running and absorbing the information in the podcast; however, you can't do both simultaneously. So leave your earbuds at home to concentrate on running. When you get home, listen to the podcast while sitting still. This is Zen.

***

In sport, the implications of Zen are important when learning a new skill, or tweaking an old one. If we give ourselves three things to focus on during a single trial, our mind will either choose one of the three, or it will become too overwhelmed and not focus on any. Therefore, it's best to attempt changing one thing per trial.

If you insist, you can try altering two aspects of a single trial, but be sure they are in progressive order. For example, if you are trying to add a few miles per hour to your throwing speed, you can say to yourself:

Bring my leg up higher on the wind-up...

Then follow through with my thumb down.

This way, the focus can switch halfway through the trial and you can be conscious of both changes. This is Zen.

YOU ARE NOT YOUR THOUGHTS

I often ask people if they meditate and many respond with, "Oh, no. I can't meditate. My mind won't stop thinking."

My response is, "Oh, you mean you're human?"

Eliminating thoughts is not the goal of meditation. It may be a nice side effect, but it's not the goal. Even the Zen masters have numerous thoughts; however, they are conscious of them and are good at organizing them.

To help organize your thoughts, put them into folders. For example, you will most likely have a folder called *work*. If you are a younger athlete, that folder will be called *school*. Whenever a thought about work or school comes up, you can place it into that folder, then carry on with what you are doing.

Over time, you will construct a filing cabinet with a number of folders, and sub-folders, which sorts your thoughts. You can begin this process by doing the following:

1. Sit with your eyes closed and use an anchor such as the breath to focus on.

2. Once you become aware of a thought, examine it.

3. Create a folder for that thought if you haven't already.

4. File it.

5. Come back to the breath.

6. Repeat.

After doing this exercise for a few weeks, you will be much more aware of your thoughts. This is the goal of meditation.

Now, you will be able to see if your thoughts provide any value. I know one thing is for sure: the vast majority of my thoughts get filed under *G*, for *Garbage*. Only at odd times does something of meaning come up that requires me to take action.

***

Once you become more aware of your thoughts, the next layer is to understand what they are. Thoughts are simply mental formations created by consciousness. They have no real substance, coming and going as the clock ticks. In other words, there are no tangible files and folders.

Over time, experienced meditators break this down, learning that the filing cabinet they've created isn't of much worth. This helps them understand *who they are*, or should I say *who they aren't*. They've learned through meditation that they themselves are not the thoughts that run through their head.

This is a challenging but important distinction to make in sport, since the inner voice that runs through our head is not the athlete performing. For the athletes I coach, I tell them to treat the voice in their head as if it's their inner coach. I encourage them to get along with their coach, and listen carefully when their coach speaks. The goal here is the same as meditation—to become more aware. This helps to *keep thinking separate from doing*.

DEVELOP AN EXTRAORDINARY MIND

According to meditation teacher Ayya Khema, "An extraordinary mind is one that can direct itself to where it wants to go." There is no doubt that having power over your own mind during competition will separate you from the pack.

There are three ways to improve focus:

While meditating.

While performing daily tasks and hobbies.

While playing sport.

By practicing all three, they will feed off each other. Soon, you will notice yourself in focus for the majority of the day. Stick with this training for long periods of time and you will develop an extraordinary mind.

TAKEAWAYS

➤ Practice meditation for sport. Use an app or other resource to get you over the hump.

➤ Find something that motivates you to continue meditating.

➤ Intentionally stick out your tongue to boost concentration and relax your jaw.

➤ Practice *lion's breath*.

➤ Read a book or watch a movie to enhance and extend your focus.

➤ Concentrate while doing daily tasks to improve your mindfulness.

➤ Do one thing at a time.

➤ Take note of your thoughts and file them. Understand that your thoughts are not who you are.

➤ Develop an extraordinary mind.

4

USE YOUR EYES, NOT YOUR HEAD

LOOK IT IN

When I was young, my dad taught me how to catch using a little plastic football in the backyard. Luckily for me, my dad was an all-Canadian wide receiver for the University of Manitoba Bisons, so he knew a thing or two about catching. He instructed me to "always watch the ball into my hands" so it wouldn't fall through what he called, "the ol' bread basket."

His words still ring in my head, "Look it in, always look it in."

***

You will see this error time and time again in professional football, where the receiver has already made their next move before making the catch, resulting in a dropped pass. Potentially the receiver had fear of getting run over by a defender, or their sights were already set on getting into the end zone. Regardless of the reason, the eyes came off the ball early and caused the error. But if the receiver had looked the ball into their hands, they'd be guaranteed to make the grab.

GET OUT OF YOUR HEAD AND INTO YOUR EYES

When we use our eyes to focus, there is little room for self-talk. Let me expand…

We know that we are best served to focus on something in the present moment while we compete in sport. To do that, we need an anchor, or something to keep our mind in that place. In meditation, that anchor is typically the breath. In ball sports, we can certainly use the breath, and I encourage my athletes to use it between plays, however I've found vision to be the best anchor immediately before and during play. When our eyes are focused on the ball, our minds can't think about the past or future. We know this because the human mind can only do one thing at a time. The instant we turn our attention to *seeing the ball*, we are *out of our head*.

Rafael Nadal said in his book, "I was so focused, I had no sense at all." His intense focus came from his eyes, and in those moments, thinking could not exist. As a result, he was playing out of his mind.

KEEP YOUR HEAD DOWN

Question:

> *In your very first round of golf, what's the first tip you get from Mom or Dad?*

Answer:

> *Keep your head down.*

This tip usually leads to decent contacts on the ball during early stages of learning. It helps to avoid the clean whiff that can commonly occur in our first kick at the golf cat. This should be the only tip you receive for your entire first round, but by the third hole, instructions usually evolve toward the knee, hip, shoulder, or elbow. Focusing on body parts not only makes the motion more awkward, but the concentration we previously had with our eyes on the ball is lost. Performance goes down.

Hitting a bucket of balls on the practice tee is the best place to play around with body parts, while simple cues like *keep your head down* should be at the centre of attention while on the links.

WATCH THE BALL

Question:

> *What's the most common instruction given to a young child learning to hit a ball with a baseball bat?*

Answer:

> *Watch the ball.*

Given this advice, the youngster locates the ball as it's held in the instructor's hand. When the ball is tossed, BINGO, the bat connects with the ball as it flies over the tosser's head. Success occurred because placing the eyes on the ball helped to make good contact on the sweet spot of the bat.

Although the youngster has early success from this tip, instructional cues often evolve toward an onslaught of information that's difficult for young brains to comprehend—or even adult brains, for that matter. Performance deteriorates.

The old adage *watch the ball* becomes lost or forgotten as the years go by.

***

In professional baseball, pitchers are hurling the ball at incredible speeds. Watching the ball, however, is still money in the bank. Let's go into detail...

To start with, the ball is hidden in the pitcher's glove. The batter should be aware of this and be gently focused on the glove. The focus is starting to narrow at this time. Immediately after the pitcher winds up, the ball becomes visible in the hand. The batter should dial in their focus even more to find it. Once the ball is released from the hand, the batter should have maximum focus, doing their best to see it as it travels through the air toward home plate. If they can get a good look at the ball, BINGO, the ball sails over the fence.

***

Let's go into more detail...

A study by Mann, Spratford, and Abernethy revealed that the best cricket batters in the world don't actually see the ball throughout the flight path because it travels too fast to be fully *tracked*. For this reason, most expert batters don't see the ball on contact.

Interestingly, however, the study found that expert batters coupled the rotation of their head with the movement of the ball. This head movement allows the expert to get a good eyeshot of the ball somewhere close to the bat. This is why the expert has more success than a novice, because inexperienced batters take their eyes off the ball well before contact. Expert batters are able to locate the ball somewhere close to the contact point.

***

Eye-work has become complicated in many ball sports like baseball and cricket. The problem with making it complex is that it increases thinking, which leads to poor results. So if you are a batter, keep things simple; approach eye-work by watching the ball with focus. It not only helps you see the ball better, but quiets your mind.

IT REALLY WORKS

Novak Djokovic is one of the best returners the game of tennis has ever seen. When you watch him closely prior to returning serve, you'll see something interesting with his eyes. He first stares at the ground for a second or two, then lifts his head and looks across the net at his opponent. When he looks across, he opens his eyes big and wide for a second, before returning them back to their natural state. This is a part of his mental routine. It requires conscious attention, which silences thinking and prepares his eyes to see serves that regularly come in at over 200 km./hr.

***

A student of mine, Dan, showed up for a Saturday morning tennis lesson complaining about his recent struggles with the return. I served a few balls at him and sure enough, he missed the majority of returns.

We met at the net to discuss and he said, "I think I'm taking it too late." It's possible that he was late on the ball, but I didn't want him thinking about this.

Instead, I wanted him to focus, so I told him to "zero in on the ball after I tossed it in the air." After contact, he was to "try to locate the ball somewhere along its flight path." He agreed to try it out.

In the next round of serves, Dan struck all but one perfectly into the court. When we met at the net this time, he said, "Man, that really works." It worked because he not only saw the ball better, but his focus on the ball did not allow for any thinking, particularly about technique, which ruins short-term results.

Watching the ball is a cue that is simple to use, but difficult to master because, next time around, your mind will want to problem-solve rather than focus.

IT'S A GAME-CHANGER

I spent a week in Calgary with the Mount Royal University women's volleyball team. On one of the days, I did some work with their serve receivers.

To start off, I had the athletes line up on the end-line of the court. I asked them to find a detail on the far wall that they could use to focus on. Then, they were to put their arms out in front of their body as if they were about to receive a serve. I instructed them to move their eyes as quickly as possible from the detail on the far wall to their forearms. This was the first drill of three.

You can do this drill at home by doing the following:

1. Sit in a chair facing a window.

2. Place an object on the windowsill.

3. Focus on an object in the distance. Focus intently on it.

4. Quickly move your eyes to the object on the windowsill. Focus intently.

5. Repeat, increasing the speed at which you move from object to object.

When you do this drill, you'll notice that there is a slight delay in the first few repetitions when moving your vision. But as you continue, the delay gets shorter and shorter. And with regular practice, you can speed up your vision so that the delay becomes almost instantaneous.

Following the first drill with the Mount Royal serve receivers, we added a ball. The servers were instructed to send in slow serves to the receiver. The receiver's goal was to narrow their focus on the ball when it was tossed up, then watch it in detail as it travelled through the air toward their arms. Then make a perfect pass to the setter. Since the ball was traveling slowly in this drill, it was easy for the receivers to *track the ball* from the server's hand into their arms.

In the third and final drill, we progressed to game-like serves by adding velocity on the ball. Now, it was difficult if not impossible to track the ball. But although they couldn't track it, they could now see the ball in more detail as it contacted the server's hand, and then at one particular instance along the flight path. Hopefully this instance is somewhere close to their arms.

The results were impressive. The receivers were consistently putting the ball on target. Why? Because prior to that day, their focus was most likely broad. But now, they had the ability to narrow it. Not to mention… there was no thinking, just watching.

To end, I called the group in to get feedback. A few of the comments were:

> *"I've never been able to control the ball so well."*

> *"Everyone always talks about eye-work, but I've never been taught how to do it."*

> *"This is a game-changer."*

Improving your vision is indeed a game-changer, so be sure that eye-work is a part of your training program. This is another arrow in your quiver.

PRACTICE EYE-WORK

Many years ago, I brought an old doubles partner Jon out of retirement to play with me in a tennis tournament. He hadn't played in a dog's age, so we lined up a practice match to catch him up to speed. During the match, he repeatedly said just that—that he couldn't catch up to the speed of the ball. Jon's a firefighter, and stays fit, so movement was not much of an issue. But his ability to see objects that travel quickly was a little rusty. He repeatedly said, "Lody, everything feels great except for my eyes. I can't see the ball."

Eventually, Jon's eyes caught up to the speed of the ball. However, if he had performed a few eye-work drills prior to the match, this would be a shortcut to getting his eyes moving again. Eye-work drills are beneficial because we can get a high number of repetitions in a short period of time.

***

NHL goalie Braden Holtby is a Stanley Cup winner who's well known for his pregame routine. He has a detailed schedule beginning first thing in the morning to prepare his mind and body. One segment of his routine is doing eye-work drills. He sits on the bench before the game and moves his eyes around the rink. He quickly moves them left, right, up, down, and in circles. He focuses on various objects, shifting his attention as fast as possible.

Other NHL goalies do similar drills, such as throwing a tennis ball against the wall and catching it. This develops speed and quickness in the eyes and hands.

Table tennis is another popular activity in the locker room of NHL teams. This is also an effective way to warm up and train the eyes, priming goalies to see slapshots that travel at speeds up to 170 km/hr.

***

The beauty of practicing eye-work is that it only takes a few minutes and you get results immediately. Technical changes can take days, weeks, or even months, but you'll see improvement in your eyes after only a handful of reps. I don't know about you, but this is the learning I want to see.

GROW EYES IN THE BACK OF YOUR HEAD

Skaters in hockey require a different type of focus. As they carry the puck, they need a more general focus, aware of everything going on around them. If they focus intently on the puck with their head down, then they will miss the open pass or defender charging at them.

It was said that Wayne Gretzky had eyes in the back of his head, but what he really had was exceptional *peripheral vision*. He combined this with a great ability to use his other senses, like hearing, to know how much time and space were available. This enabled him to always hit the open man, amassing an unbelievable 1,963 assists in his career.

***

In volleyball, peripheral vision is important for blockers so they can see the ball, the setter, and attackers coming in at different angles. There's a lot going on in a short period of time, so having good peripheral vision allows them to see everything.

In basketball, point guards need to see the ball in their periphery while they watch the other nine athletes move around the court. Excellent peripheral vision would be an advantage for an athlete that plays this position.

***

If peripheral vision is a requirement in your sport, it can be practiced by doing the following:

1. Sit in a chair and focus on an object straight ahead.

2. Keep your eyes on that object while you become aware of various things in your periphery.

3. See how far to the left you can see objects while keeping your eyes looking straight ahead.

4. Then see how far to the right you can see objects.

5. Then up.

6. Then down.

Train your eyes according to the demands of your sport. *General* eye training will help, but *specific* eye training will be the real game-changer.

GET INTERESTED

In the 2010 Stanley Cup playoffs, the Philadelphia Flyers and Chicago Blackhawks were squaring off in game six of a best-of-seven series. The game went into overtime with the Blackhawks up 3-2 in the series.

During the intermission, *Coach's Corner* with Don Cherry and Ron MacLean came on the air. They did their usual five-minute segment (mostly filled with Cherry ranting), and culminated with Ron MacLean's routine question, "Who are you picking to score the OT winner?"

Cherry immediately replied, "Patrick Kane... He looks interested."

Sure enough, only four minutes into overtime, Kane scored the Stanley Cup winning goal. So the question is:

> *How did Cherry know?*

The answer:

> *He must have seen concentration in Kane's eyes.*

***

The opposite of being interested is *tanking*, which is an attitude of *I don't give a shit anymore*. If you find yourself falling into this mental trap, include the words "get interested" as guidance-talk in your mental routine. These words are a signal to focus on what you see. Ideal focus here consists of the eyes *relaxed*, but *dialed in*. In other words, *soft*, but *alert* —like a predator. Now, you are engaged, ready to score your OT winner.

USE YOUR TIME WISELY

One athlete, Emily (who you will meet later in the book), told me once that she would train her eyes using license plates as her mom drove her to games. This is a great use of time, not only because it warmed up her eyes before the game, but because this is an opportune time for her mind to run rampant around outcomes of the upcoming game.

Remember what Andy Puddicombe said: "Focus doesn't know pressure." In Emily's situation, while she was focused on license plates, pressure did not exist. In other words, she was *in her eyes* and not *in her head*.

TAKEAWAYS

➢ Use your eyes as an anchor immediately before and during play. This will improve your vision and quiet your mind.

➢ Watch the ball when performing skills like catching, hitting a golf ball, batting a baseball, returning a tennis serve, or receiving a volleyball serve.

➢ Improve your peripheral vision if you are a playmaker in hockey, a point guard in basketball, or a blocker in volleyball.

➢ Practice eye-work according to the visual demands of your sport.

➢ Warm up your eyes prior to a competition.

➢ Be interested while competing. Do this by keeping your eyes soft and alert.

➢ Use eye-work to silence thinking before a big competition.

5

VISUALIZE SUCCESS

IMAGES ARE BETTER THAN WORDS

While teaching with the University of Winnipeg, I chaperoned a group of twenty-five students with a fellow teacher named Charlotte on a trip to Costa Rica. We stayed in a small town in the mountains called Llano Bonito, with a population of only 2,000 people. It was uncomfortably hot, all day, every day, but it was a great experience because the local people that hosted us were so friendly and accommodating. We were there to work with the community on various projects around town, one of which was building small greenhouses to grow plants for food.

On the first day of work, we were introduced to a few men that were in charge of the project. Since they spoke little to no English, the men went straight to work with no instructions or job briefing after being introduced. The students were a little confused, looking around as if they should be receiving instructions of some sort. A few of them asked Charlotte and me what to do and all we could do was shrug our shoulders.

After the students watched for a while, they started putting their hands in. There were few, if any, words exchanged between the students and the local men. They communicated mostly via sounds and gestures, with the odd "aqui" (meaning "here") to indicate where something was supposed to go.

Impressively, by the second day, many of the students were building greenhouses on their own. If they ran into trouble, they would walk over to look at the first greenhouse that was built, then go back to theirs to tackle the problem. Because I'm interested in the process of human learning, I found it neat to see how quickly these students learned with practically no verbal instructions.

***

This is a great lesson for skill acquisition in sport. To learn a new skill, we first need to see it done properly. Since humans are naturally copycats, we can reenact the image we've created in our mind.

As a young coach, I spent enormous amounts of time using words to explain how to perform skills, followed by feelings of frustration when the athletes couldn't do them. Over time, I learned that words are a waste of time if there is no image linked to them.

Timothy Gallwey says, "Images are better than words," so when learning a new skill, use pictures and videos. This creates a visual in your mind of exactly how the skill should be performed. Then you have a template for your subconscious mind to copy.

YOU HAVE TO SEE IT TO BELIEVE IT

I taught a large class of 130 students at the University of Manitoba. The course was *motor learning* and I wanted to show the students the power of video in acquiring skill. I used the tennis serve to show them.

I had the students congregate at the university tennis courts at Max Bell Centre. When they arrived, I handed out their assignment. On day one of two, they were to pair up with a partner and record each other serving a handful of balls from different angles. I gave them no technical instructions at all as they got to work.

Their homework over the next week was to analyze their videos. To do that, they were instructed to download their videos onto their computers and set them up to play on half the screen. On the other half of the screen, they were to choose a tennis professional of their choice and play videos of them serving. They were instructed to compare their serve with their chosen pro, noting any similarities or differences. They were also told not to watch any videos that had verbal instructions on how to serve.

A week later, we met at the courts for day two. The students performed another round of serves. Same exercise as day one; however, their next bit of homework was slightly different. They were to set up another split screen, but this time, half the screen was their first round of serves and the other half was their second round of serves. That way they could evaluate if any changes had been made from the video analysis they did during the week.

As the second session ended and I began packing up the racquets and balls, I glanced over and saw a student perform the smoothest serve I'd seen either day. The ball traveled perfectly over the net and into the court with pace and spin. I said "wow" as she turned around and smiled at me. As soon as she looked at me, I recognized her face from the first session. Although there were 130 students sandwiched onto three courts at once, I remembered her day-one serve, which was nothing like the serve I'd just seen. I said to her, "Woah, your serve really improved—what did you do?" She responded by saying that she thought this assignment was really cool and how she planned to incorporate video analysis with the young athletes she was coaching in gymnastics. She then chuckled as she told me she had spent way too much time over the past week watching YouTube, and not studying for exams. She also mentioned that these were the only tennis serves she'd ever done. How's that for proof that video analysis works?

In the next lecture, many other students spoke up in astonishment about how much improvement had been made without any verbal instruction, or doing any actual reps of the skill. Although the students didn't perform *actual reps*, they received *mental reps* (provided they did their homework). When those students showed up to serve on day two, the desired movement pattern had been imprinted into their brains and was ready for replication. They now knew only one way to serve—like a pro.

***

Use your phone as a tool—to film and watch yourself perform the various skills in your sport. Watch the videos in detail, then spend time watching the pros in your sport to see what they are doing. Write down a list of things you notice, then go out and practice. Repeat the process.

By doing this exercise, you are not only creating the proper mental images, but you are becoming a student of your sport. When you take control of your own learning, and have some success, it's empowering. Not only that, you now have the knowledge to teach others. Just be sure to use your words carefully.

TAKE MENTAL PICTURES

During one year of coaching volleyball, our school hired a photographer to take pictures of the players for the school's website and promotions. The photographer took hundreds of action shots. After scrolling through them, I saw something interesting…

Our best serve receiver had her thumbs perfectly in line as the ball contacted her forearms. The other athletes' thumbs were slightly apart, overlapped, or misaligned.

We've all heard the phrase *it's a game of inches*, and this is definitely true of the forearm pass in volleyball. If the platform is slightly out of line, even by half an inch, it can change where the ball will travel. But with a perfect platform, athletes feel more confident in the contact. The result is a cleaner and more controlled touch on the ball.

Next practice, in our meeting room, I showed the team the photos and explained the optimal platform. The still photos I showed them on the projector created mental pictures in their brains, which were now ready for imitation. Off we went to practice.

After a few weeks, the athletes raved about how much better these minor adjustments felt. And in our next tournament, the changes we made showed up on the stats sheet with a big improvement in our serve receive numbers.

*****

We know that creating mental videos in our mind is an extremely effective way to acquire or change a skill. We can also use still images to capture a specific detail that's important. Once we have that image, we can practice with it in mind. Eventually, we do it without thinking.

HAVE YOU HAD YOUR MOMENTITO?

On my second trip to Costa Rica as a chaperone, our group did a hike. When we arrived at our destination (an incredible waterfall), I overheard our Spanish-speaking tour guide say the word "momentito." I'm not sure why the word jumped out at me. Maybe because it had a good ring to it? Or maybe because the word *moment* was familiar?

A few days later, I heard it again. So I asked Charlotte, who was well versed in Spanish, what it meant. She said it meant "a little moment." It's common in Costa Rican culture to locate little moments. They are characterized by:

Awareness.

Stillness.

Joy.

It's a feeling as if time is standing still.

For the rest of the trip, the word caught on. Whenever Charlotte or I had a little moment, we would shout out "momentito!" and have a little chuckle.

***

Years later, I had a momentito while doing a Vipassana course. I was walking in the forest during a break when things started popping out at me in much greater detail. The sights and sounds of the forest were creating a sensation overload as I stumbled upon an ant hill. Instead of walking by, like I usually did, I got down on all fours and observed it from about a foot away. There were thousands of ants all busy at work. I would find one particular ant and watch it closely to see what it was doing. I was fascinated, as if I was a kid again, which brought a big smile to my face.

It was a moment filled with awareness, stillness, and joy.

Time stood still.

***

Momentitos can occur in sport. I experienced one while I was completing a master's degree at the University of Victoria. One of the required courses was *sport psychology*, taught by a retired field hockey professional named Veronica. Her lesson plans were a little helter-skelter and difficult to comprehend through the thickness of her strong Argentinian accent, but her passion and energy for the mental side of sport were clear.

She had us do an activity called *guided imagery* where we sat at our desks, closed our eyes, and imagined her words as she calmly and gracefully spoke to us. Her tone of voice was as if she was trying to hypnotize the class. It went·something like this:

"Imagine yourself in competition...

Imagine the sun shining...

Feel the heat of its rays beating down on you...

Listen to the sound of the crowd...

Listen to the sound of the whistle...

Observe the feeling of a perfectly struck ball traveling into the net for a goal...

Enjoy the sights and sounds of celebration."

It was clear that Veronica was reflecting on her experiences in field hockey, but I made the connection with my sports—specifically, tennis. I imagined a few shots hitting the sweet spot of my racquet, smack-dab in the middle of the strings, and how nice that feels.

This was the first time I'd done any form of *visualization* for sport in all my years of playing and coaching. Veronica told us this exercise can have a powerful impact on the athletes that we coach. She added that we should consider implementing it into our training programs. I remember thinking to myself that although this activity was a nice opportunity to relax in class, it wasn't something I'd incorporate into the teams I coached since it was a bit "out there" for high school and university athletes.

Only a few days later, I experienced what Veronica was trying to describe...

In a doubles tennis match, I served a ball and came to the net. Our opponent hit a screaming forehand back, but luckily it was right at me, so I just put my racquet in front of my chest in self-defense. The ball hit squarely on the sweet spot. It felt as if the ball was absorbed by the strings, paused there for a second, then fired out like a slingshot. The ball travelled back to the returner just as fast as he sent it to me. It caught him completely by surprise and he botched the next shot.

***

To this day, I've never had a feeling like that, where time seemingly stopped as the ball was held on my strings. I often replay that moment in my mind to recreate that unique encounter.

Momentitos may seem pointless to someone who hasn't experienced one. However, they can have a powerful effect on one's psyche. In the short term, they can completely turn around our mindset, and in the long term, we never forget the feeling.

Look for your momentito, when the clock stops and there is nothing but awareness, stillness, and joy.

VISUALIZE TO BE THE BEST

Many years ago, I had the pleasure of coaching Darian Picklyk, who is now the top Canadian defensive player in university men's volleyball. He had a break-out year in 2021-22, amassing an amazing 209 digs in his fourth season with the University of Winnipeg Wesmen. This total was head and shoulders above the rest of the league.

When Darian met with head coach Larry MacKay after the season, Larry asked him what he did that season to get to the next level. Darian said he set a goal:

To be the best.

He knew that all top athletes did something off the court to enhance their performance on the court, so he turned to imagery. He spent time reading books and watching documentaries about imagery, and came up with a routine for games and practices.

To prepare for a practice, Darian opens up his journal and writes down how he wants to perform that day, including aspects of the game he wants to improve. He then closes his eyes to visualize it. Altogether, his practice preparation takes him about eight to ten minutes to write down and rehearse the desired actions.

During practice, while the backup libero gets reps, Darian is off to the side of the court going through the motions as if he was performing them. He calls these *fake reps*; however, the benefits of doing this are very *real*.

After practice, Darian goes back into his journal to reflect. He remembers some of the key plays that stuck out in his mind and in particular the mistakes he made. He spends a few minutes fixing the errors. He finds this to be an extremely effective way of correcting bad habits because they seem to naturally evolve to the way he visualizes them.

The key for Darian is to be *intentional* in his visualization, to see the finest of details on the technical side of the game. He rehearses his mental videos in slow motion so his mind can clearly see the proper way to perform the skill. He also makes sure to always visualize skills performed correctly. If he imagines them done incorrectly, he quickly hits rewind and replays the video with a positive process and outcome.

It's also important to note that Darian's visualization practice comes from his own eyes, which is referred to as *first person visualization*. We can also perform imagery from a *third person* perspective, where you watch yourself perform as if it's seen through a camera. Although Darian uses first person, research has proven both to be effective for different situations. To keep it simple, choose the one that works for you and feel free to switch back and forth.

Toward the end of my conversation with Darian, he added that it's just as important to visualize the mental components of volleyball. To do this, he sees himself:

Communicating effectively on the floor.

Being a good teammate.

Keeping his emotions in check.

He also told me he imagines his team losing, then fighting back to win. This way it doesn't feel foreign when the Wesmen get down a few points. He can remain optimistic about a comeback.

Developing this routine proved to be Darian's turning point, helping him become the top backcourt player in the nation.

Not only was coach MacKay interested in what Darian was doing, but his teammates wanted in on his secret weapon. So Darian taught his teammates. They began meeting in their team-room prior to games to set their minds straight. They would make sure the room was quiet with the lights turned out. The players would close their eyes as Darian led them through a guided imagery session. Here is a sample:

> *"Matt goes back to serve and rips a jump-serve down the line for an ace...*
>
> *The set goes out to Daniel and he lays in a perfect off-speed tip over the middle blocker's hands and onto the floor."*

Darian was going through what's called a *script*, where words are spoken aloud to guide actions in the mind. Note that his script contains very detailed actions, and always ends with a positive result.

Imagery as a pregame mental tool helped the Wesmen finish the year first in the CanWest East division. With Darian back for one more year, they are visualizing another successful season in 2022-23.

MULTI-SENSORY VISUALIZATION

When entering into a pressure-filled competition, we come in with an enormous advantage if we have experience competing in that particular event. If we've been there before, we know what to expect. If we've never been in that environment, our mind senses danger as we build up to the competition since there's fear of the unknown.

***

Alex Honnold became well known for his free solo ascent of El Capitan in Yosemite National Park in 2017. A *free solo climb* is done without any ropes, harnesses, or protective gear. When Honnold was interviewed on *The Jay Leno Show* shortly after his incredible feat, Leno asked how climbing one of the world's toughest rock faces without any protection wasn't terrifying.

Honnold said he had spent an enormous amount of time visualizing the climb while living out of his van, memorizing each and every move within that pressure environment. When it came time to get on the rock wall, it was like he had done it thousands of times, so he was able to do it without any fear.

***

It's difficult, if not impossible, to replicate pressure situations in practice; however, you can use visualization to anticipate the setting. Engage all the senses, such as sights, sounds, smells, and feelings that you might expect in that environment. This is called *multi-sensory visualization,* which will prepare you well for challenging circumstances.

VISUALIZE PERFECTION

Ed Mylett asked Phil Mickelson, "What separates the fiftieth guy on tour from the top few guys on tour?"

Mickelson responded with, "The ability to visualize or see shots before they happen." He went on to say that the top golfers "visualize perfection." They have the ability to see things in great detail, whereas many of the lower ranked golfers on tour aren't able to get as clear a picture.

When Mickelson sustained an injury that kept him off the links, instead of taking a holiday, he worked hard on rehab and shot a round of golf every day in his living room. He held the club in his hands while imagining and feeling each shot within a round.

When he returned from his injury, he played really well in his first round because he had been practicing. Not only was he practicing, but practicing perfection, by visualizing every shot exactly the way he wanted.

***

We can get quality repetitions in our sport by closing our eyes and imagining what we want. When done properly, these mental reps are just as valuable as actual reps. In some cases, they are even more valuable because:

→ We control the outcome.

→ We consume less physical energy.

→ We can slow down skills to see more minute details.

→ We can imagine them while under pressure.

MAKE A HIGHLIGHT REEL

Construct a highlight reel of your best moments in sport using video. Once it's assembled, you'll have a confidence-building tool to use before a competition.

You may not have the time or resources to put together an actual video. If that's the case, do it mentally by going through the following steps:

1. Write down a list of your best moments in sport.

2. Place your list in front of you, close your eyes, and take a deep breath.

3. Open your eyes to look at your first highlight.

4. Close your eyes and replay the moment.

5. Open your eyes and look at your second highlight.

6. Close your eyes and replay that moment.

7. Repeat the process for the remaining highlights.

This tool is endorsed by David Nurse, who coaches NBA stars on the mental side of basketball. Nurse says that over 80 percent of our self-talk thoughts are negative, but by using a highlight reel, "our self-talk pivots from negative to positive."

START WITH THE OUTCOME

Another way to practice visualization is to work backward in the execution of a skill. This is called *end-point visualization.*

To use this tool, start by imagining a successful outcome. Then use your rewind and pause buttons to see how you got to that point. Every time you hit your pause button, take a photo in your mind to capture that phase. Let's use a three-point shot in basketball as an example:

1. See the ball swishing perfectly through the mesh. See where you are at this moment.

2. See the ball at its highest point in the shot. Notice your body in the air with your wrist following through.

3. Feel the ball in your hands as you load up the shot.

4. See yourself making a pass or dribble fake to open up the shot.

5. Watch yourself coming off a screen to get open and receive the ball.

***

End-point visualization is not only effective for individual skills, but for an entire competition. To do this, start by visualizing yourself after a performance. See yourself enjoying victory or reacting to a loss in an appropriate way. Then work backward, all the way to the start of the day. Visualize yourself with the right demeanour at each stage and take mental photos of these moments.

Once you get into the real competition, and one of the photos you previously took becomes a reality, this will be a really cool moment. Tennis icon Andre Agassi called his Wimbledon triumph in 1992 "a déjà vu experience," since he'd already won it in his head so many times. So close your eyes and conceptualize success. The more you can do this, the better chance your wish will come true.

TAKEAWAYS

> When learning something new, spend time watching videos of how the skill should be performed. Practice the skill with this in mind. Words can be used later to recall the images.

> Look for moments in your sport where there is complete awareness, stillness, and joy.

> Practice visualization. Close your eyes and imagine the physical and mental skills of your sport being performed the proper way.

> Use multi-sensory visualization (sights, sounds, smells, feelings) to place yourself in challenging environments within your sport.

> Visualize perfection. If it's not perfect, hit rewind and try again.

> Make a highlight reel to replay your best moments in sport.

> Try end-point visualization. Start with the outcome and work backward through the process.

> Visualize yourself achieving your ultimate goal.

PART TWO
MINDSET

*"Whether you think you can or
you think you can't, you're right."*
—Henry Ford

6

HAVE GRIT

PLAY WITH HEART

Growing up, I was the smallest kid in class for what seemed like forever. I didn't hit my growth spurt until my first year of university. The junior high years were the toughest because I was bullied regularly, and this taught me to run away when fear presented itself. Perhaps this is why I became a runner, competing in cross-country, track, and eventually marathons. However, I was always running away from what was behind me, rather than toward what was in front of me.

This mindset stayed with me into my twenties, particularly when I played sports. When pressure arose, my fight-or-flight response was activated, and I always chose flight.

Although I lacked fight from early childhood, I've been fortunate to have a tennis partner who carries a boat-load of it. Let me tell you a few stories about Stephen's determination...

One year, he was in the singles final of the Victoria Beach tournament against Patrick, a young Jedi on the court at the time. They found themselves in a third and final set, which became a grind in the mid-summer heat. Stephen won a few tough points to earn himself a match point. Before lining up for the return, he put his hand up to pause the game and walked over to the next court and threw up.

In a situation where many athletes would stop play and maybe ask for a fifteen minute injury time-out, Stephen treated it like he had to sneeze. Without hesitation, he walked back onto centre court, nodded at Patrick to serve the ball, and won the point and match.

***

That same summer, Stephen was in another grueling singles match in Winnipeg against Evan—a rangy redhead who plays like a human backboard where every shot comes back at you the same way you sent it. The match carried on into the wee hours of the night. A few of us battled the mosquitos and stuck around for the conclusion.

Toward the end of the match, Stephen was battling cramps, particularly in his racquet hand. In the middle of an important point, his racquet flew out of his hand and slid across the court. Evan recognized this and simply lobbed the ball back into play. Meanwhile, Stephen ran over, picked up his racquet, and continued the rally for another handful of shots.

In this situation, many athletes would have watched their racquet sail across the court and given up on the point. This was not in Stephen's nature. Although he lost that crazy point, and the match, it was an epic battle that I will always remember.

***

Stephen and I have competed as doubles partners for over twenty years. During that time, there is one match that stands out in my memory. We were playing Kirby and Patrick and started the first set down 5-1. Nothing was going right.

We were next up to serve, so I said to Stephen, "Let's try to win this game so that when Patrick holds, we can serve first to start the next set." Although I was attempting to be optimistic about us holding serve, I was waving the white towel on Patrick's serve and the possibility of a first set comeback.

Stephen looked at me in disbelief, and shouted, "We're not losing this set!" (with some added profanities that I'll leave out of the book). This was the spark we needed. We went on to win the next six games in a row to take the first set, 7-5. From there, we kept the momentum rolling, winning the second set and match... thanks to the kick in the ass Stephen gave me when I wanted to roll over and play dead.

***

If you are lacking courage in sport, you can improve it by surrounding yourself with, or observing those that have it. Choose an athlete in your sport that you admire and competes with a high level of grit. It can be an athlete that you play with, or against. It can even be a professional athlete that you watch on television. Study the way they play, particularly their body language and facial expressions. Once you have a clear understanding of their mindset, go out and replicate it.

Vince Lombardi said, "If you're lucky enough to find a guy with a lot of head and a lot of heart, he's never going to come off the field second." So *use your head*, and *play with heart*.

BE DRIVEN

Having coached youth sports for many years, I've seen numerous young athletes that possess drive. These individuals have the ability to face a challenge head-on by furrowing their brow and saying, "Come on, let's do this!"

One such athlete is Akash.

In Akash's ninth grade year, she was devastated when she found out she didn't make the senior team. Rightfully so, since she was certainly good enough, but we wanted her to stay back on the junior team. Instead of throwing in the towel that season, she worked really hard to improve her game.

The following year, she showed up determined to make the senior team. She not only made the team, but became an immediate force to be reckoned with. In our last game, Akash hit the final ball out of bounds, ending our season. Unfortunately she felt our loss was all her fault. This was because she was competitive, and had a hard time letting this go. I'm sure she replayed that point over in her head hundreds of times. Regardless, Akash was on her way to achieving big things in the sport of volleyball.

Things took an unexpected turn in the off-season before her grade eleven year. She woke in the middle of the night and ran into her parents' bedroom screaming at the top of her lungs. She frantically told her parents that her head felt like it was going to explode, so they rushed her into emergency.

Later, she underwent surgery that involved cutting open her skull. The surgery went well and thankfully, the doctors saved her life, but she had a long road to recovery.

When I met with her a few months later, she insisted on playing volleyball in the upcoming season. I could see on her face that this was non-negotiable. Sure enough, she was ready to go on day one. She ended up having a great season, but was still not satisfied when we got smoked in the provincial final.

Prior to her graduating year, Akash worked extra hard off the court since she still had two goals she wanted to achieve:

To win a provincial championship.

To play post-secondary.

In her final season, she found herself in a provincial championship rematch with the same team as the year before. Up 14-12 in the fifth set, with two match points, everyone in the gym knew where the ball was going. She put the final nail in the coffin by smacking a kill to take home the gold medal and tournament MVP honours.

Shortly after, she received a volleyball scholarship to the University of British Columbia, fulfilling her second goal.

Akash's road has no doubt been a tough one, but her perseverance through tough times is the reason she's accomplished so much. Instead of running away from challenges, she faces them head-on.

DIG IN

On the evening of the sixth day of my ten-day meditation course, there was a posting on the bulletin board just outside the meditation hall that read:

Day 7: Adhitthana (Strong Determination)

Vipassana courses have three mandatory group sits per day, during which everyone meets in the meditation hall for more formal meditation periods. On Adhitthana day, we were asked to sit in one position for all three one-hour sessions. We weren't to flinch a muscle, open an eye, or make a peep.

That night, before Adhitthana, I had an especially hard time sleeping in anticipation of the upcoming challenge. I was afraid that the back pain that presented itself over the past day or so would become even worse if I wasn't able to adjust my posture.

The next morning, during the first sit, the low back pain reared its ugly head as expected. I gave in and changed postures. I tried to mentally reset, but repeatedly gave in to the urge to readjust my position.

In the second sit, same thing.

Immediately before the third sitting, I said to myself, *I am going to achieve this goal, even if they have to carry me off on a stretcher.*

It turned out to be one of the most challenging hours of my life. I had to push through piercing pain, but I achieved my goal. I will never forget the last few minutes of that hour. The entire room, filled with about fifty people, was completely quiet and still—like Gallwey's glass lake. All I could hear was a faint ringing in my ears, the subtle sounds of breathing, and a gentle wind whistling through the window. It was a feeling of achievement and fulfillment. And I must confess, I moved a few muscles... I couldn't help smiling.

***

Although it seems as though Adhitthana is designed to torture, that is not the intention. The goal of Adhittana is to grow determination, which can be used in other areas of life, specifically sport.

Determination helps us when it's time to dig in, which leaves us with feelings of pride and self-satisfaction when we come through.

This is what we play for.

HOW BADLY DO YOU WANT IT?

One year, a volleyball team I coached squeaked our way into provincials; however, we were outmatched in the tournament from start to finish. We ended up finishing fourteenth out of sixteen teams. After our last match, with the season over, we stuck around to watch the finals. It turned out to be an excellent match in a great atmosphere.

After the finals, we got on the team bus and the girls were in awe. One said, "That was so amazing."

Another said, "They're so good."

Since we were a young team at the time, I responded with, "You can be there one day, but the question is, *how badly do you want it?*"

At that point, the athletes were faced with a fork in the road. They could continue to play volleyball recreationally, or they could make volleyball their priority and passion by setting some lofty goals. As it turned out, they chose the latter.

Over the next few years, they did everything they could to improve. They joined club teams, attended numerous camps and clinics, played beach volleyball, and hit the weight room. Some athletes dove into the mental skills you are reading about in this book.

Three years later, they were not only in the final, but were crowned provincial champions.

Michael Jordan said of the Bulls' championship run, "All we needed was one little match to start that whole fire." For this group, watching the provincial final three years earlier was the match that sparked their fire. Once they had a fire going in their belly, they were motivated to put forth the immense amount of time and effort required to be champions.

***

I learned a few things from this group. One, that a motivated mind is powerful, but when a group of minds have a similar interest, the power isn't added, it multiplies exponentially. Two, when a group puts forth an immense amount of effort, and it pays off in the end, there is no better feeling in the world.

This is what we play for.

Take a look at your ultimate goal. Ask yourself:

How badly do I want it?

IT TAKES GUTS

One of the hottest fads in the self-help world is cryotherapy, or cold exposure, popularized by Wim Hof (also known as *The Iceman* for his ability to withstand freezing cold temperatures). Wim tells us to take a cold shower—or, better yet, to fully immerse ourselves in cold water. After we do this, we feel great, not only because of the physiological benefits of cryotherapy, but because we accomplished something that is hard.

Challenge yourself by attempting things that are difficult. This will build character, giving you the guts you need to take on the extreme demands of your sport.

JUST GO

One day, I had a random thought. I had coached high school volleyball for almost twenty years and felt like I had heard the words *call the ball* a gazillion times. Whenever a ball dropped on the floor between two or more players, everyone would yell out (sometimes in unison), "Call the ball!" I often joined in on the chorus, but it dawned on me that day that the issue may not be *calling the ball*, but *going after the ball*.

I came up with a new phrase for our team:

Just go.

I wanted the word *just* in front of *go* so the athletes could understand the simplicity in it. Going for the ball is the only thing they had to do. It was not necessary for them to call it, or think about any technical or tactical cues. They just had to go.

Our team that year didn't have much height at the net, so we had to be tough on the ground. So I was envisioning an environment where all six athletes on the court were relentless in keeping the ball off the floor. This new environment was hard for the athletes early on, since it required effort and sacrifice, not only in games but in practices. They collected numerous bloody knees and bruised hips to show for it.

It took some time, but after belting out a few hundred *just go's*, we started to really pursue the ball. The words became contagious within the team, and the parents as well. Toward the end of the season, I overheard an athlete from another team say, "Oh, that's the team that digs everything" in reference to us. We were frustrating to play against, thanks to a simple cue that shifted our mindset from *your ball* to *my ball*.

Back-row defense in volleyball is mainly a mindset. More specifically, a *gritty* mindset. Is there an area of your sport that requires this attitude? If so, just go!

NEVER GIVE AN INCH

Early on in another season of coaching volleyball, we were winning matches but were digging ourselves into a hole at the beginning of every set. We'd find ourselves down, 4-1, or 7-2, and would have to claw our way back to win the set.

In a mental skills session, I brought up this issue. One of the athletes had an idea from one of her previous teams—to use the phrase:

Race to ten.

At the start of every set, we would set a mini-goal: *to beat our opponents to ten points*. Whether or not we achieved this goal, we would then focus on getting to twenty-five. Everyone on the team liked the idea, so we went ahead with it.

In our next tournament, I had our coaching staff watch the beginning of each set closely. They informed me after the tournament that we had beaten every team to ten points in every set! This was interesting to me because there were no technical or tactical changes; the only difference was paying more attention to the early stages of a set using a phrase that increased our effort level.

Race to ten later evolved into *race to five, race to fifteen, race to twenty* (or any other number that seemed fitting for the situation). This cue not only gave us a better start, but divided the game into smaller, more manageable pieces.

***

For our upcoming zone championship, I put Natalie in charge of deciding what we were going to race to. Natalie was a player with lots of knowledge, but was reluctant to speak-up in team huddles. My hope was that this job would get her more involved as a leader.

In our semi-final match, Natalie set the race to ten points before the start of the match. Despite this, we found ourselves quickly down, 8-0. Feeling the heat, I called time-out. At the end of the time-out, I looked at Natalie and said, "Race to fifteen?"

Natalie looked at me in disappointment and replied, "No, race to ten!"

Amazingly, we went back onto the court and before I knew it we were up 10-9! We went on to win the match.

This was a lesson for me—*to never give the opponent an inch*. Not two points. Not even one point.

DON'T BE COMPLACENT

Imagine you are a hockey player and your team jumps out to a 4-0 lead in the first period. The natural instinct is to ease off the gas pedal. This is a mindset of *complacency*, which is the opposite of *determination*.

If your opponent is stubborn, and you sit back and relax, before you know it the score is 4-3 after two periods of hockey. Your opponent now has the momentum going into the third period.

Your team is in panic mode during the intermission, which is also an ineffective mindset.

In the third period, your opponent completes the comeback with a 5-4 victory.

***

Although this was a tough loss, hopefully you and your team learned from this experience. Let's hit the rewind button back to the first period...

While you were filling the net with pucks, you could have changed your mindset by changing the score. For example, once the score became 4-0, you could have told yourself and your teammates that "the score is 2-2." Combine this with a determination cue such as "pedal to the metal" and you'll find that your effort level stays high. You stay *interested*.

As the game continues, keep reminding yourself and your team of a score that will keep you strong-willed and persistent. Before you know it, the horn goes and you've given your opponent a good ol' fashion beat-down.

BELIEVE IN YOURSELF

Our volleyball team experienced a turning point mid-season one year when an athlete sent me a video. It was a short documentary about the Stanford University women's volleyball team, who began their season with low expectations since their team was mainly rookies. As the season progressed; however, the team found momentum and eventually caught fire. Toward the end of the year, Stanford shocked everyone by winning the national championship.

In the documentary, head coach John Dunning was interviewed after the championship game. He said, "When a team that doesn't think they're that good starts to believe, it becomes like a snowball rolling downhill. The more snow that piles on over time, the more momentum. Toward the end, we had a ton of momentum, and we truly believed we were gonna win today. It didn't matter what got in our way."

I watched the video a few more times and picked up on the key word—*believe*. The more I thought about it, the more I realized that our team didn't truly believe we could win—we were only *hoping* we could win. We needed a way to get our snowball rolling downhill, and this needed to come from a change in our mindset.

I forwarded the video to the team and told them to be sure to watch it before our next practice.

In our pre-practice meeting, I told the team that I questioned whether or not we truly believed in ourselves. The look on their faces was a bit defensive, but after more discussion, they started to see what I was seeing. Believing became the focus of attention from that point on. In order to build it, we would say "believe" before every team cheer. I also made a conscious effort to say the words "believe in yourselves" as often as possible. This new mindset became a part of our culture, giving us the confidence we needed to be successful that year.

***

At the end of our journey, the team gave me a little present—a stone carving of the word *believe*. It sat on my mantle for a few years to remind me of what I learned that season:

To always believe in myself.

It was a sad day when the carving fell and shattered into pieces. I thought about trying to glue it back together, but refrained from doing so because I realized that *belief isn't something you hold in your hand, it's held inside.* The experience was the real gift the team gave me.

TURN HOPE INTO BELIEF

Michael Jordan dominated the NBA throughout his career and his success was in large part due to his determination and belief. Jordan said at the end of *The Last Dance*, "It all starts with hope."

When we say to ourselves, "I hope I can _____," we are *wanting* to accomplish a goal. We may have reasonable confidence that one day we'll achieve that goal, but we don't *truly believe* it will happen. Jordan is right: it starts with hope, but eventually we need full conviction that we can accomplish our ultimate goal.

Our level of belief can fall somewhere along the following continuum:

→ No hope—"I can't do it."

→ A little hope—"I don't think I can do it."

→ Hope—"I think I can do it."

→ Conviction—"I know I can do it."

If you are currently near the top of this continuum, you will naturally progress down by simply participating in your sport. This progression is typically slow, but we can accelerate this process by having grit. With this mindset, we step on the gas pedal, practicing harder and more often. We become like the little engine that could—*I think I can, I think I can...*

Soon, we find ourselves at the bottom of this continuum, truly believing in ourselves and having deep conviction that we *can* do it. That's when dreams become tangible.

ANYTHING IS POSSIBLE

Nepalese climber Nims Purja set out on an unprecedented mission—to climb fourteen 8,000+-metre mountains in only seven months. Everyone in the climbing community said it was impossible, which is why Nims named the mission *Project Possible*. Believing was clearly his mindset.

Nims achieved this impressive feat by finishing all fourteen peaks in six months and six days, proving all the naysayers wrong. In the documentary *14 Peaks*, his opening line was, "Don't be afraid to dream big," and toward the end of the documentary, he said, "The world is learning."

We certainly did learn from Nims— *to dream big.*

OVERCOME ADVERSITY

I coached Kate in volleyball for three years. She was passionate about the setting position and had high hopes to be our starting setter going into her Grade 12 year. However, she lacked the agility and athleticism required for this position.

As the season started, a younger setter was performing well so Kate was becoming less optimistic about her goal. I think she was having thoughts of quitting. She asked me one day after practice if we could chat. I knew right away what it was about.

When we met, I confirmed with her that the younger setter was indeed outperforming her. She had a look of deflation. I didn't want to see her leave our team, so at the end of the meeting I proposed an idea...

One of our middles had been struggling with her serve, so I told Kate that we would need someone to take on the role of serving for this athlete. The job would not only be to serve, but play defense, every time that athlete came around.

This is a difficult role because the substitute has to come off the bench, ice cold, and perform. I also told her how important this job was—since this player controlled a twelfth of the game (based on six servers per team). The few points this individual served and defended could determine the outcome of a close game.

I offered her the role and she was somewhat intrigued, but wanted some time to think about it.

When she arrived at practice the next day, she had a smile on her face. After a few minutes of warming up, she approached me to say she'd be happy to take on the role. Later that practice, when she was not in the drill, I looked over and saw Kate serving against the curtain.

The next day, I was walking by the racquetball courts at lunch hour and saw Kate practicing her serve against the wall. I smiled, happy that Kate had found her niche within the team.

Kate's serve improved dramatically over the next month and she became a weapon for us. However, her defense needed work, especially since she had a bad habit of digging the ball with one arm. Digging with one arm can be effective in an emergency situation, but not when the ball is within an arm's reach and traveling at a reasonable speed. I felt like a broken record, shouting out the words "two hands" to her more times than I can remember.

One day, I told Kate about a coach that tied his athletes arms together while he hit balls at them. I had no intention of doing this, but when I finished telling her this, she looked at me square in the eye and said, "Let's do it!"

The next day, I met her over lunch hour and we tied her arms together using rubber tubing. I hit balls at her while she worked on keeping both arms together.

***

Fast forward to the provincial championship, which took place in the small town of Virden, Manitoba. We worked our way through the draw and into the finals against the host town. The crowd was hostile as the match swayed back and forth, landing at 13-13 in the deciding set. Guess who's turn it was to serve? Yup, you guessed it—Kate's.

As she subbed in, I could sense how nervous she was. She tentatively lobbed the ball into play. We were lucky to win the point on an attacking error, going up 14-13. We now had a match point. Virden called time-out.

In the huddle, I told Kate we needed a tougher serve and to trust her training. She went back out and hit a tough serve into play. Not only that, but their attack was hit to her right side and she stuck both arms out to get the dig that set up the winning kill.

After we celebrated as a team, Kate came running up to me and yelled, "Two hands!!!" It was as if to say "I finally got it!!!" It was a moment I will never forget, and certainly one she won't either. To an onlooker, it would be perceived as *a pretty good serve* and *an OK dig*, but we both knew there was so much more behind those two contacts.

***

Kate faced adversity early in the season, but with adversity comes opportunity… an opportunity to reroute.

Since this experience, I've proposed this role to numerous athletes and some have turned it down. They'd rather sit on the bench. But not Kate. She refused to throw in the towel and embraced the opportunity.

Sometimes we get rerouted from our original dream. The key is to *keep dreaming*.

TAKEAWAYS

➤ Observe those that exhibit a great deal of determination in your sport and replicate their traits in your game.

➤ When faced with a challenge, dig in and go for it.

➤ Challenge yourself by doing things that are hard.

➤ Take a look at your ultimate goal in sport and ask yourself, how badly do I want it?

➤ Never give your opponent an inch. Fight tooth and nail for everything.

➤ Never run away from a challenge. Face it head-on and always believe it can be done.

➤ Dream big.

➤ Sometimes you'll get re-routed from your original dream. Don't stop dreaming.

7

BUILD CONFIDENCE

SOW THE SEED

When I teach full-day volleyball camps, I like to break up the day by providing the athletes with some motivation. For that, I tell the story of Jack, which goes something like this...

Years ago, I was hired to coach a sixteen-and-under boys' provincial volleyball team. When Jack walked in the door for the first Saturday morning tryout, my initial thought was: *he must be the younger brother of one of the athletes*. When he started putting on his shoes and knee pads, I realized he was actually trying out!

Halfway through practice, Jack still looked half asleep with morning bed-head. He also wasn't able to tread water in a few of the attacking and blocking drills because of his size. For those reasons, I crossed him off my list of athletes that could make the final roster.

Three tryouts later, however, Jack had grown on me. I had to erase the pencil line I stroked through his name on day one. He grew on me because he had a great attitude and always played with a smile on his face.

On top of that, since the tryouts were mostly scrimmages, I kept track of individual points. Shockingly, Jack was at the top of the leaderboard. *How could that be*? I thought to myself... *He must be doing something right.*

I combined this with the fact that I wasn't overly excited about the other setters trying out, and decided to go on a hunch and keep him as our backup setter.

We traveled to Edmonton for Nationals and in the first few matches our starting setter was faltering. He didn't look comfortable, most likely from the added pressure of the competition. Jack stepped in. Much like tryouts, he didn't do anything flashy, but distributed the ball to the right hitter at the right time. And still with a smile on his face.

Entering playoffs, it felt strange having Jack as our starting setter because he was a foot shorter than the rest of the team. However, he continued to run the offense well in crunch-time. Our team played great with Jack at the helm and we captured the bronze medal, which was an excellent result for our squad. Jack left that team with an extra big smile on his face. It was clear that his confidence was growing.

The story continues…

The following club season, I was asked to coach a seventeen-and-under team. Since it was Jack's age group, I made sure he attended tryouts.

When he showed up, he had grown a few inches and put on some muscle mass by hitting the weight room—a much different look than the previous spring. He was also developing into a great setter, training every morning before school at the University of Manitoba, which was an hour drive each way from his home in Lockport, Manitoba.

Although things were falling into place for Jack, there was still a problem with his game. He was susceptible when blocking. Teams knew his weakness so they would take advantage of it by hitting the ball hard down the line when he was in the front row. Despite this, he was good enough to be our starting setter.

Midway through the season, we had a two-hour bus ride from Winnipeg to Brandon. I had some time to think. I wondered why Jack was still ineffective at the net despite having the size to get his hands above the tape. *Could this be in his mind?*… I thought to myself… *Maybe he's holding onto a lack of confidence from previous seasons?*

I called Jack up to the front of the bus to have a chat. I told him, "You aren't 'the little setter' anymore. You're bigger and stronger now, so expectations at the net are no different for you than the rest of the team." He smiled and nodded as he usually did. As he walked to the back of the bus, my initial thought was that this chat was a complete waste of time. Boy, was I wrong.

Jack led our team that tournament with eight solo stuff blocks! This is a remarkable stat for a setter at the seventeen and under level, and particularly for Jack, since up to that point in his career he probably only had one or two total.

His eighth block was the best of them all. It was in the first set of the finals and the score was 23-all. Our opponent did what we expected, setting the ball toward Jack and hitting the ball hard down the line. However, Jack was ready for the task and dished out his biggest rejection of the bunch. He turned and looked back at the team with his fist in the air and a look of sheer confidence.

After we won the next point to close out the first set, I looked over at Jack's mom and she was practically in tears. Seeing this put a lump in my throat. If you were to ask me why I coach... this is why.

That weekend was Jack's coming-out party as he sowed the seed of confidence. Many years have passed since then, and he is now completing his final year as the starting setter for the University of Manitoba Bisons. He recently entered the top ten list in Canada West history for assists, an achievement that seemed way out of reach for him at a young age.

From this story, we can learn a few things:

→ One, *never let genetics get in the way of achieving what we want.* The mind is much more powerful than size or stature.

→ Two, *confidence can grow.* In some cases, such as Jack's, it can grow like a weed.

CONFIDENCE VERSUS FEAR

As a big fan of *Seinfeld*, I've seen all the episodes; many of them more than once. If you aren't a fan, the early episodes start with Jerry doing a short standup comedy set. In one particular episode, he does a routine about public speaking. His punch-line joke goes, "The only thing that people fear more than death is public speaking... so you're telling me that people would rather be in the casket than reading the eulogy?" This sounds ridiculous, but we've all felt the nerves that coincide with public speaking, making it easy to relate to this joke.

Performing in front of the mic is similar to performing in sport because all eyes are on you. We get those gut-wrenching feelings that are uncomfortable, impeding our ability to perform at our best. These feelings stem from fear.

Climber Nims Purja said, "The biggest strength I have is I have no fear," and Rafael Nadal said, "It is the player who manages to isolate himself best from his fears who ends up being number one." To isolate ourselves from *fear*, we need to build *confidence,* since the two are inversely proportional. Once we own confidence, like Nims and Nadal, fear is removed so we can perform at the apex of our sport.

TAKE IT HARD TO THE HOLE

Stephen Curry is one of the most dominant players to ever play NBA basketball. Listed at a generous six-foot-one, he fears nobody when he goes to the rim. In game six of the 2022 NBA finals, Curry was rejected early in the game as he drove to the hoop for a layup. The ball went out of bounds and his team retained possession with plenty of time on the shot clock. When the camera panned to him, the look on his face was stone cold, like nothing happened. He then took an inbound pass and went straight back to the hole, dishing off to a teammate for a basket. That game, Curry ended up with thirty-four points as he led his Golden State Warriors to another NBA title.

For many players, getting blocked early in a game would take a chomp out of their confidence, but it was hardly a hiccup for Curry as he retained the high level of courage he always brings to the court.

OVERCONFIDENCE

In many cases, we approach sport with a lack of confidence. This can come in the form of worry, nerves, or being overly cautious. On the other side of the coin, we can approach a performance with overconfidence. The thinking here is that *this will be too easy* and is often characterized by arrogance, bragging, or taunting.

Playing with too much swagger is better than playing anxious, but there are problems with it too. When we approach a competition in this way, it's all fine and dandy when things are going well, but when problems arise, there's more turbulence because it's unexpected. When *I have this in the bag* turns into *uh oh, I could lose this*, the mental image we've created for ourselves becomes jeopardized. As a result, we start to panic. This often leads to a shattering of confidence as fear takes over.

A key to performing at our best is in holding confidence. Once we find it, it's important we don't overfill the boat, because if we spring a leak, we're guaranteed to sink.

THE SCALING TOOL

When I met with expert mental performance coach Andrei Mandzuk, I explained to him one of my favourite coaching tools—*ranking things out of ten*. For example, one year, I regularly asked my athletes to rank their confidence level out of ten, both individually and as a team. I allowed negative numbers (which indicated fear) and numbers above ten (which indicated overconfidence). It was important that we, the coaching staff, didn't provide any help with the numbers or give them any feedback. This is because we only wanted *awareness of what currently is*. We didn't consciously try to change anything.

Timothy Gallwey said "awareness is curative" in *The Inner Game of Tennis,* and he was right. Our numbers gradually went up over time with heightened awareness.

***

After I told this story to Andrei, he told me that this exercise is called *scaling* in the world of mental performance. Here are a few tips to get the most out of the scaling tool:

→ Be sure to make it a regular habit.

→ You can do it verbally or by recording the numbers in a logbook.

→ It can be done individually, as a team, or both.

→ It can be scaled out of twenty, if that's preferred.

→ It's best to come up with your numbers without thinking for too long.

Think of a number right now between one and ten that depicts your current confidence level in sport. Revisit this number every day for the next month to see what happens to it. Most likely it will go up, naturally, because awareness is curative. The result is competing with a higher level of confidence and a lower amount of fear.

Andy Puddicombe says, "It's not about being free of fear, it's about knowing it intimately." By scaling confidence, we get to know our fears.

CONFIDENCE SWINGS

Once you become more aware of your confidence, you'll see how quickly it can change. I saw this one match where we came in with the expectation to win. We started off great, jumping out to an early lead. Our opponents called a time-out and we came into the huddle with a *we've got this in the bag* mentality. I was also overconfident, laughing at one point in the time-out. Big mistake.

We went back onto the court and proceeded to lose a long string of points. This time, I was the one to call time-out. As the athletes came into the huddle, I couldn't believe my eyes. In less than ten minutes, laughter and swagger turned to angst and panic. In other words, a plummeting on the confidence scale. Fortunately, we were able to weather the storm and bring our confidence level back up to close out the match victorious. More important than the win; however, we learned that:

Confidence is volatile.

***

Approach every competition with the same level of confidence, regardless of the opponent and what's at stake. This is half the battle. Keeping the needle from moving too far in either direction is the other half. To prevent the needle from wavering, regularly check-in with your confidence during competition. This will keep you in a good range.

THE CONFIDENCE SWEET SPOT

Once you start seeing confidence in yourself, you will see it in others. When watching sports on television, evaluate the confidence levels of professional athletes by watching closely as the camera zooms in on their face. Try to scale it out of ten. Then see if it changes as the event wears on.

***

During the Tokyo 2021 Summer Olympics, the men's indoor volleyball had a most unexpected result. France, who came into the tournament as a middle-of-the-pack team, squeaked their way into the play-offs by finishing fourth in their pool of six teams.

In the playoffs, they started to heat up as they upset Poland in the quarter-final. They then knocked off Argentina in the semi-final, and finally, shocked Russia by defeating them in the final. Going into that final match, Russia clearly had more size and skill, but France found the confidence sweet spot. This was clear by the looks on their faces, especially their leader, Earvin N'Gapeth, who exudes confidence.

An old coach of mine, Rob Svenson, used to say "ride the wave" when things were going well. This is exactly what France did, they caught the perfect wave and rode it all the way to shore. They found themselves on the podium with gold medals wrapped around their necks and masks over their faces, but this didn't hide the immense amount of confidence they brought up there.

HIGH-VALUE PLAYS

In sport, certain plays are worth more than one point psychologically. These *high-value plays* can escalate (or deplete) confidence levels. At the level I coach volleyball, big blocks tend to have the highest value. The bigger the block, the more demoralizing it can be for the athlete or team.

I discovered this in a playoff game when our team got blocked twice in the first three points of the match. It took me until we were down 6-1 to call time-out. When I looked at the facial expressions of our athletes as they came into the huddle, it looked as if they wanted to go home.

Sure enough, we never moved past the initial shock as we proceeded to tip and roll the ball over the net time and time again. These are actions that are typical of underconfidence. In the end, we lost a match that we shouldn't have, thanks to an early knock to our confidence.

***

At our next practice, we talked about the match as a group. Since we were competing in a team sport, we had the advantage of being able to work together to address the issue. One athlete came up with a great idea—*to improve our block coverage.* In other words, when one of our athletes went up to swing, the other five players would surround the athlete in case the attacker got blocked. It didn't sound like much when she first said it, but it really grew on me since it would give our hitters a feeling of security; a feeling of *my teammates have my back.*

Although block coverage is a skill, it translates to the mental game.

For the next few practices, we paid attention to improving our block coverage, coming up with plans and systems for which defenders would cover which attackers. We also had everyone yell "Swing!" when the coverage was well set up. This gave our hitters the green light, freeing them from the shackles of fear. If the ball happened to get blocked down onto our side, we would applaud our opponent, but nothing more. Next point, it was back to business, remaining fearless.

***

Knowing the high-value plays in your sport is important for two reasons:

1. We can learn to manage high-value plays when they happen to us.

2. We can place greater emphasis on practicing these skills to inflict them on our opponent.

We know that confidence levels can quickly sway back and forth, so it doesn't take much to turn momentum in, or out, of our favour. But by placing an emphasis on high-value plays, momentum stays on our side.

THE HUMAN CONDITION

Michael Phelps, winner of an unbelievable twenty-three Olympic gold medals, was interviewed by Mike Tirico immediately after the Olympic Games. Phelps said, "Competing at this level was really overwhelming; all we want is someone to talk to. We just want someone who listens and doesn't want to fix us."

Talking is one of the best ways to investigate the anxieties that come with sport, and Phelps knew this. When we talk about our fears, it has a way of diminishing them, releasing the pent up energy to the outside world.

***

Before a practice with one of my volleyball teams, I set up a circle of chairs in the middle of the room. When the athletes came in and sat down, I asked them the question:

What's your biggest fear?

They were free to think for a few minutes and jot down any notes. Then I gave each athlete a turn to speak. It turned into a powerful exercise because we put our fears into the open. It was also refreshing to hear that everyone had worries. A feeling of, *Hmm, I'm not the only one.*

This is referred to as *the human condition* by Andy Puddicombe on Headspace. It refers to the idea that we are not alone when we face challenges in life. If we are struggling, we should remind ourselves that there are others with the same condition, and many that are much worse off.

Talking about our fears seemed to ease some of the tension as we entered the playoffs. It gave us the feeling that we could work together as a team to extinguish our fears, making way for confidence.

***

Paul Maurice, who previously coached the Winnipeg Jets, knew the importance of communicating with his players. Therefore, he made a conscious effort to have regular, meaningful conversations with each and every player, not only about hockey, but life.

As an athlete, make a conscious effort to talk, as difficult as it may be, to the people around you. This builds confidence.

MAKE A MANTRA

Nowadays in my coaching, I allot a significant amount of time and attention to mental training. From this, I've learned that a surprisingly high number of athletes carry a lack of confidence into competition. They may look confident, or express confidence, but inside there is fear. Fear of what? *Fear of failure.* This needs to be addressed because it clearly compromises performance.

To address fear, *Mantra statements* (which is a form of positive self-talk) is a tool we can use to override anxiety. If you practice yoga, you are familiar with the word *Om*. It's often chanted near the beginning of a class. Holding the *mmm* sound creates a vibration in the body that can help calm the mind, increase attention, and improve mood. Om dates back to before 1000 BC, when early yogis found them to be a weapon of supernatural power. Over time, Om evolved into more elaborate phrases that became known as mantras (also referred to as *positive affirmations*). They are used for self-assurance and motivation.

When silently repeating positive phrases to oneself with eyes closed, this is called *transcendental meditation,* or *TM*. This practice began in India in the mid-1950s and was later popularized by Herbert Benson in his book, *The Relaxation Response.*

Om, mantras, and TM are all designed to build confidence, which tackles negativity, self-doubt, and fear.

***

Many of today's coaches are using mantras with their athletes. One such coach, Anson Dorrance, uses them to build confidence in his female soccer players. Dorrance is one of the most successful sport coaches of all time, compiling an incredible twenty-one NCAA championships in his last thirty-one years of coaching at the University of North Carolina.

At the beginning of every season, Dorrance helps each athlete construct an elaborate statement that is meaningful to them. The process is ongoing, with constant adding, deleting, and editing of the statement. Athletes memorize it and recite it to themselves at suitable times.

One year, I took a page out of Dorrance's book by having my athletes build a mantra statement. Checking in with their statement became a part of our pre-practice mental routine. I would also give them a reminder to say it to themselves at fitting times, such as before games and during time-outs. When we did this, it seemed to prime us to compete with more audacity.

***

A friend of mine completed his first half marathon using the mantra "I am automatic." It related to the fact that every challenge he sets his mind to, he accomplishes. He said, "Does this sound arrogant when I say it out loud? Yes. But is that a problem when its purpose is to motivate and give me confidence in the middle of my running battle? No." He highlighted the fact that it was a phrase for him, and only him. Nobody else needed to know.

***

Mantra statements are used to convince ourselves that we are capable. This is because, when used regularly, the words and their meaning become imprinted into our brains. For this reason, adding a mantra is a nice addition to your growing stack of mental tools.

Here are some examples that could be a good starting point in building your own mantra:

> *I am capable of anything that I put my mind to.*
>
> *I honour and respect myself.*
>
> *I choose faith over fear.*
>
> *I am powerful.*
>
> *I will triumph over all challenges that come my way.*

Once built, repeat your mantra to yourself a few minutes per day. Soon, negative self-talk becomes obsolete and your confidence will be sky-high.

HIT IT HARD

When I was teaching motor learning at the University of Manitoba, I stumbled upon a fascinating study on hockey players shooting the puck. A large group of subjects was divided into two—an A group and a B group. Both groups were given the same amount of practice time; however, the instructions they received were different:

→ Group A was told to shoot the puck as hard as they could, not worrying about where the puck went (even though there were targets set out in the goal).

→ Group B was told to focus solely on hitting the targets, without any attention to the speed of the puck (even though there was a radar gun recording the speeds).

When it came time to test the participants, subjects were tested on both the *speed* and *accuracy* of their shot. As expected, group A scored higher on the radar gun for puck speed, but what was fascinating was that group A also scored higher on the accuracy test. But why?

One theory is that group A participants developed confidence in their ability to shoot the puck, which was key when the new element of accuracy was added. The B group, when told that speed was also being tested, tried to apply more force but didn't have confidence in that motion.

The implications of this study are:

> *If you are young, or just starting out in a sport, focus on generating power.*

This develops confidence in the action. The accuracy will come later, oftentimes naturally.

***

I've seen the impressive results of using this learning strategy while growing up as a junior tennis player in Manitoba. One particular athlete was taught to hit the ball hard. He lost most of his matches at a young age to players that simply lobbed the ball into play. But once he found his accuracy, he started hitting everyone off the court. His opponents, who *played it safe* for so many years, had a tougher time learning to hit the ball hard later in life because they didn't have certainty in the swing.

The *hard first strategy* can be used for any skill where speed and accuracy on a ball or object is essential. Skills such as:

> *Throwing a football.*
>
> *Throwing a baseball.*
>
> *Spiking or serving a volleyball.*

Smashing a badminton bird.

Kicking a soccer ball.

JUST BREATHE

The Iceman, Wim Hof, not only endorses cold water exposure but raves about the benefits of *breath-work*, which is a new trend in the world of sport. To do Wim's breathing technique, do the following:

1. Lie down on your back and get comfortable.

2. Hyperventilate yourself with thirty full breaths done rapidly.

3. Then hold your breath for as long as you can after the thirtieth exhale (at low lung volume).

4. Next, breathe in and hold your breath at the top of the inhale (high lung volume).

5. Repeat this process three times and do the exercise daily (ideally under supervision if you are young or trying it out for the first time).

According to the Wim Hof official website, if this breathing exercise is done daily, and combined with cold water exposure, it:

Boosts energy levels.

Is a natural anti-inflammatory.

Stimulates better sleep.

Aids recovery.

Increases sport performance.

Relieves stress.

Boosts concentration.

Increases happiness.

***

When I first started doing this form of breath-work, I found it difficult to hold my breath for more than forty-five seconds. There was definitely some underlying fear of what may happen if I held it too long. Because of my unease with the procedure, I wasn't able to calm my nervous system, which is a benefit that is commonly experienced in others.

After a few months of practicing, however, it became more comfortable. And soon, I was able to hold my breath for an extended period of time.

One day, I decided to do Wim's breathing technique with exactness. I ended up doing it for about ten days in a row. At the end of the ten days, the biggest thing I noticed was a huge spike in confidence. When I walked down the street, I'd strike up conversations with almost anyone that went by. I didn't care if they ignored me because I had a feeling of excitement to be alive. And on the tennis court, I was hitting the ball without hesitation. I felt fearless.

Since Wim Hof breathing was a confidence builder for me, and has been for so many other athletes, try it out. Or experiment with another breathing technique to find the one you like.

The bottom line?

Just breathe.

TAKEAWAYS

- ➤ Grow confidence to tackle fear.

- ➤ Find the confidence sweet spot with the scaling tool.

- ➤ Approach every competition with the same level of confidence, regardless of your opponent.

- ➤ Check in with your confidence level throughout a competition.

- ➤ Pay attention to high-value plays in your sport. Learn to manage them when they happen to you and put an emphasis on handing them to your opponent.

- ➤ Make an effort to have meaningful conversations with the people around you about your fears.

- ➤ Build and recite a mantra statement.

- ➤ If you are young, or early on in training, focus on generating speed and power.

- ➤ Use breath-work like the Wim Hof technique to build confidence.

8

BALANCE YOUR MIND

BUILD THE BRAIN YOU WANT

After I moved to Vancouver, one of the seven jobs I accumulated was teaching *biomechanics* in the School of Kinesiology at the University of British Columbia. The content was a bit physics- and math-rich for my blood, and not sporty enough. I often got side-tracked from the content by telling stories about my experiences as an athlete and coach. The students found the stories more interesting than doing calculations, but it wasn't giving them what they needed. By the end of the course, I knew this wasn't the right fit.

On the last day, I told the class that my next venture was "to explore the mind." At that point in life, I hadn't discovered the power of mental training. But that year, I developed an inkling that bettering the mind was more powerful than calculating angles.

I wasn't exactly sure how I would begin this exploration, but nevertheless, a few days later, I sat down to start.

I began by watching YouTube videos on the anatomy of the brain. This is not necessarily the best way to delve into the mind; however, it got the ball rolling and linked me to an interesting TED talk by Lara Boyd. Boyd was ironically doing brain research out of UBC. She was studying *neuroplasticity*, which is the ability of the nervous system to change by developing new neural connections. Boyd said that we are constantly adding new wiring to our brain, even as we age. It was refreshing to hear from Boyd that we have an enormous amount of control over the happenings between our ears.

I loved her last line of the talk, which was:

"Go out and build the brain you want."

This is certainly relevant for sport, since building a powerhouse brain gives us dominance over the competition. So let's get to work!

UNDERSTAND IMPERMANENCE

Studies in neuroplasticity affirm what the Buddha discovered centuries ago—that all things in the universe are constantly changing. The Vipassana word for this is *anicca*, or *impermanence*.

On day four of a ten-day course, Anapana switches to Vipassana, where, instead of the breath, attention is turned to the body. Instructions are to scan the body, moving the attention up and down, feeling for sensations and observing their changing nature.

After a few hundred body scans, I started to grasp what was meant by anicca. Subtle sensations, such as the itch on my brow, would be gone within minutes. In the evening discourse (which is a video to help meditators learn the Vipassana technique), the teacher, S.N. Goenka, said, "No itch is eternal." This put the itch situation into perspective. Regardless of whether I scratched it, it would eventually be gone.

Even the crudest sensations, such as my intense lower back pain, felt different every time I scanned through because experiences at any one moment are fleeting.

This is anicca.

***

Emotions, such as anger, are also transient. When something infuriates us, it will slowly start to dissipate. And after a few minutes, it's possible we are completely back to normal.

I've felt this change many times when taking my dog for a walk. As a puppy, Rudy would often do things that would frustrate me. However, as we kept walking, that frustration would quickly turn to joy if he did something cute. I may even find myself laughing at his playful humour a short time later. This laughter is now an enjoyable feeling, but it also won't last forever. Anger will be back at some point in the future, and so will joy.

This is anicca.

***

Impermanence has ties to sport. For example, we can get stuck holding onto concrete mindsets such as *I'm a worrie*r or *I have confidence issues.* We speak these words like they're a characteristic of ours that never changes, like we're stuck with these characteristics for life.

We may also give ourselves a label such as *I'm a choke*r when we fail to deliver under pressure a few times. If we give ourselves this label, there is no doubt we will choke again. Instead, we should say:

> *I choked a few times. Next time around, my mind will be different.*

This is understanding impermanence, which gives us a fresh opportunity to deliver the goods. Who knows, maybe we will find the zone and throw-down a work of art. Then, we certainly aren't "a choker."

BUILD AN EQUANIMOUS MIND

Once we understand that thoughts and feelings are fluid, we can establish more balance in our mind. The Vipassana word for this is *equanimity,* which is defined by Merriam-Webster as:

> *Evenness of mind especially under stress.*

This is the objective of Vipassana—to balance the mind by staying equanimous toward the various body sensations that we experience.

***

In 2019, Stephen and I were in a semi-final doubles match and I was feeling the heat. We were losing early on to a team that we were expected to beat. With Stephen carrying me on his back, we were able to rally and win the match in the last few points.

Although we won on the scoreboard, the pressure had taken its toll on me. Immediately after shaking hands, my lower back seized, my right calf started cramping, and I was exhausted. Previously, I'd played pick-up doubles matches for hours on end and felt totally fine afterwards. So my pains couldn't have had anything to do with the physical demands of the game. They must have been caused by my mind twisting and squeezing my muscles—like wringing out a wet towel.

There were only a few hours before the final. I was barely able to bike my way home, even though it was only about a hundred metres away. I went straight to bed and lay there like a corpse. Although the muscles in my back were seizing, I told myself, "This intense sensation isn't permanent." This is equanimity, which is a mind that doesn't react in panic, but calmly observes.

I eventually dragged myself out of bed an hour later. I grabbed a bite to eat and laboured my way back to the courts for the final.

When I started warming up, I found it peculiar that I was now relaxed and composed. What was more, the pains in my body were nearly gone. My mind and body had completely changed over the course of a few hours and I ended up playing a great match.

***

In sport, we can experience a number of different emotional states and physical sensations during competition. The key is to remain equanimous with them, giving these mental and physical forms less energy. The ability to have mental harmony, or evenness of mind, is a skill that should be in every athlete's toolkit.

ACKNOWLEDGE AND ACCEPT

Novak Djokovic once said, "I acknowledge fear and accept." In other words, he becomes aware of the feelings of fear and is submissive to them. Novak doesn't fight the fear because he knows that if he reacts in dismay, it will only intensify.

***

When we repeatedly *acknowledge* and *accept* feelings and sensations as they are, they resolve over time because our bodies naturally seek homeostasis. This is learned in a ten-day Vipassana course. Even the stickiest of mental and physical feelings may seem too solidified to transform, but by repeatedly feeling them with *awareness* and *equanimity*, the ingrained pattern of the mind can be completely reversed.

BE A DETECTIVE, NOT A JUDGE

There's a common phrase used in meditation—"Every meditation hall needs a fly." Why? Because an annoying fly buzzing around a meditator can be used to learn how to deal with animosity.

Sometimes, while I'm focused in meditation, Rudy startles at something outside the window. When he barks, it creates a really unpleasant sound that pierces my brain every time. As bad as it feels, it's an opportunity to strengthen my equanimity by allowing his barking to play out. At other times, he will come over and lick my face, which is the ultimate body sensation while doing Vipassana!

Rudy is the fly in my meditation hall.

***

Although barking and face-licks are not typical situations that we come across in sport, they can be used as a tool to train our mind within a controlled setting. They are mental reps that make us more resilient to the ups and downs that will undoubtedly come our way in sport. Once we get hundreds, even thousands, of reps (like the Zen masters), we remain in stasis when shit hits the fan.

What's the fly in your meditation hall? Use your fly as a tool to train your mind to be an observer, not a discriminator. In other words, *be a detective, not a judge.*

FIND BALANCE ON THE BEAM

While we compete in sport, we walk along a balance beam. If something goes wrong, followed up by a reaction of negativity, there is a wobble to one side. On the contrary, if something good happens, followed by an overreaction of excitement, we wobble to the other side. We can make it to the other side of the beam by wobbling right, then wobbling left, then right, etc., but a better way to balance is with no wobbling at all.

When we attempt to balance on an actual beam, the first few seconds are often the hardest before we stabilize. This is similar in sport, where the early stages of a competition are usually the most difficult to find mental balance. It's a time when we have all those funky feelings of nerves and excitement, but it's crucial to stay steady here. Do this by observing what's happening in your body while keeping your cool. If your heart and breathing rates are high, just observe. If adrenaline is pumping through your veins, or your hands are shaking, just observe.

As the competition progresses, the ebbs and flows of sport will want to push you off the beam. Continue to be solid as a rock. When you maintain this mindset, you remain poised until the end of the competition, which is when you need it most.

***

Kobe Bryant said it best after Phil Jackson taught the Lakers how to meditate. He said, "We were never too high or never too low, we were just in the moment." In other words, they trained their minds to stay balanced when turbulence was felt. If they were down in a game, they didn't react with frustration. If they were up, they didn't react with hysteria. They stayed strong and let their opponent wobble. Phil, Kobe, and the Lakers knew that, in the NBA, it's the team that maintains perfect mental composure that find themselves poised at the end of the beam—victorious.

THROW 'EM AWAY

Whenever I attend sporting events, I like sitting court-side so I can listen to the coaches during time-outs. Years ago, I was watching the Brandon Bobcats women's volleyball team when head coach Lee Carter used great words to keep his athletes in mental balance. He told them to imagine that each of them had a backpack strapped around their shoulders while playing. If they made an evaluation after a play, they were to throw it away instead of putting it in their packs. Regardless of whether they had a negative or positive thought, if it went into their backpack, the weight would become too heavy to move by the end of the game. But if their backpacks were empty, they could perform at a high level.

So I will ask you:

What's in your backpack?

BE MENTALLY TOUGH

At the beginning of my coaching career over twenty-five years ago, I misunderstood what *mental toughness* meant. I thought of football players smashing helmets together prior to games in order to pump themselves up. Unfortunately, these actions will only kill brain cells, making us mentally weaker.

Instead, let's follow the lead of Andy Puddicombe, who says, "Mental toughness is about letting go." He's referring to letting go of the highs and lows of sport, which is quite the opposite of smashing heads together.

***

Let's revisit Andy's predator hunting in the wild as a nice example of mental toughness...

After an unsuccessful attempt at catching prey, the animal doesn't get frustrated and go pout under a tree. They get right back in the game by remaining patient, searching for their next attempt. When the animal locates another potential target, they are completely unaffected by the previously failed attempt because they were able to let it go. They continue with this mindset until successful. Then they are proud of themselves as they enjoy their meal, but don't dance around in celebration.

***

An old opponent of mine, Doug, was like a predator. He was arguably the best tennis player to ever play in Manitoba, moving on to compete at the top level of US college tennis.

Every summer, Doug would come home to mop the court with us, winning some tournaments with nothing but bagels the whole way through. When you "bagel" someone, you beat them by a score of 6-0, 6-0. I was on that bagel-train and it felt as if I was playing against a robot, since Doug never said a word or cracked a smile. He just took care of business, with a heart rate that likely never went above seventy beats per minute and a facial expression that said, *I can go all night.* He was an emotional rock that was difficult to budge, winning the mental battle time and time again.

WATER OFF A DUCK'S BACK

One of my favourite metaphors is *water off a duck's back* to remind athletes to remain in symmetry. When something irritates us, we can say the phrase to ourselves as we exhale the breath. The words, combined with the breath, can calm our mind and release tension in our body. This allows us to *let go*, better preparing us for the next action.

***

After I used *water off a duck's back* for a few weeks with a volleyball team, an athlete put up their hand during a team meeting and said, "Where does this saying come from anyway?" Before I could stumble through an explanation, another player jumped in to explain that the feathers of a duck are an evolutionary adaptation that helps to regulate its internal body temperature by repelling water. The feathers prevent cold water from getting absorbed into the animal's skin. I was impressed not only with this girl's knowledge of biology, but with how perfectly the words fit for sport, since:

We can't let things get under our skin.

***

In a pick-up tennis game, my partner hit a good serve and our opponents hit a feeble return to me at the net. The ball was approaching with no pace or spin, and hung in the air for what seemed like an eternity. A few possible shots went through my head during the time, none of which happened. It resulted in a missed overhead as I yelled, "*No!!!*"

Walking to the next point, I was shaking my head in shame. The next ball came to me (of course), and since I was still rattled, I butchered another volley. This gave them a break of serve that eventually cost us the match.

Let's backtrack to fix my problem...

Screaming at the top of my lungs immediately after the first error was not ideal, but these reactions are often done unconsciously and are difficult to avoid. It created a wobble on my balance beam, but I had plenty of time before the next point to reset my mind. Using a cue, such as *water off a duck's back,* could have been used to let go of the mishap. Then my mind wouldn't be hijacked by negative emotion and I'd have had a much better chance of putting away the next shot.

***

Be mentally tough by practicing letting go. You'll find that the more you practice, the quicker you'll be able to find neutrality when these circumstances next arrive at your doorstep. With prolonged practice, you won't yell *No!!!* in the first place.

USE TRIGGER WORDS

When coaching volleyball one year, I used my experience teaching high school biology (and particularly genetics and probabilities) to make a change in our team's mindset. We were having trouble digging ourselves out of holes, so in a mental skills session I held a coin in my hand. I asked the team, "If I flip this coin, what is the probability that it will land on heads?"

Everyone agreed with 50 percent. Of course they were correct, but the next question required a bit more thought. I asked, "If I flip this coin and it lands on heads five times in a row, what is the probability that it will land tails on the sixth flip?"

The majority again said 50 percent, but a few were a little unsettled with this answer. The answer is indeed 50, because each event (or flip) is independent of the previous ones.

This was relatively straightforward so far, but the discussion got a lot more interesting when I asked them, "If we lose the first five points of a match, what is the probability that we win the sixth?"

A variety of numbers were given but none of them was 50 percent or higher. I didn't have any stats at the time, but I would have agreed that our winning percentage in that scenario was less than 50.

Once we all agreed, I gave them the final question: "Why?"

The team collaborated for a while and decided that our minds were carrying feelings of disappointment and frustration into the next point. These feelings negatively affected the way we played.

At this point in the season, if we did nothing, the previously fixed mindset would continue. However, now that we were aware that the past was hindering the present, we had an opportunity to change this negative chronic response.

To break down this problem, I introduced *trigger words* into our team's vocabulary. The first athlete that recognized we were in a rut was to shout out "independent events." This would be a signal for each athlete to become aware of their mental state. This prompted us to re-balance on the beam. Each athlete was to take a breath, then place their attention on the upcoming point, treating it separately from the past.

By making an effort to make each point independent, this led to a dramatic improvement in our ability to deal with the swings of volleyball that year.

***

While competing in sport, keep an eye out for times when you get in a jam. Come up with designated words for these situations and use them the moment they start to materialize. This will help you stay out of the gutter.

KEEP YOUR COOL

My mom was very involved with and supportive of my sports, spending hours driving me from sport to sport when I was young. During car rides to practices and games, she never gave me any technical or tactical advice, but she made sure I had good sportsmanship.

I will never forget an incident when I was playing a match in a junior tennis tournament. On the court beside me, a kid was throwing his racquet over and over again. At one point, he smashed his racquet against the ground. A few moments later, his dad walked onto the court and handed him a brand new one.

After the game, my mom was infuriated. It was as if she was yelling at me, even though I hadn't done anything wrong. She cursed, "Nobody remembers who wins or loses, but they will always remember the brat who was throwing their racquet! And they sure as heck remember the dad who walked onto the court to give him another one!!"

She was spot on with this because, to this day, I don't remember if the kid won or lost his match, or even whether I won or lost my match, but I definitely remember the inappropriate antics on the next court.

At the end of the day, although I wasn't the one making the "racket," the message got through: *Don't do that.*

***

Not only are you a poor role model when you over-react in sport, but it affects your ability to perform because you've lost the balance of your mind.

The Buddha said, "A wise man is patient and is not provoked to respond in anger; like the doorpost he is firm." Tennis great Roger Federer was a wise man. He knew the importance of controlling his anger, which was exemplified by the way he acted on the court. But interestingly, Federer had frequent outrages on the court as a young athlete. At a certain point in his career, however, he was able to step back and see that his unruly behaviour was doing himself more harm than good. He was quoted as saying, "I couldn't stand watching me throw racquets and embarrass myself in front of thousands of people in a live stadium. So I tried to change." He clearly made a change.

***

Playing with mental balance doesn't mean you should play softly, or passively. Federer, for example, competed with oodles of passion and confidence. He wanted it as much as anyone on tour, but without the zany antics portrayed by many others in his sport. This allowed him to not only achieve greatness, but be remembered as a great guy.

AVOID OVER-EXCITEMENT

When I first started out coaching volleyball, I thought that celebrating after every point was important for success, so I encouraged my athletes to cheer whenever we won a point. I even got mad at them for not cheering—does that make any sense?

As I progressed as a coach, I learned that celebrating helps in the short term (with an upward swing of momentum) but always creates a steep slope on the flip-side when things start to go wrong. Our team's mental state would go up and down like a yo-yo. This is because:

*Every high has a low and every low has
a high.*

***

Imagine you are on a basketball team and are entering a game as the underdog. Your team meets in the locker room before the game and you put on the pump-up music, jumping up and down to get the juices flowing.

You start off the game with an early 10-0 lead on sheer adrenaline, but since playing under this heightened state can only be maintained for a short period of time, your opponent pulls even.

You call a time-out to get re-energized with a motivational speech from your coach, then come out and score a few quick baskets. This spike in adrenaline is weaker than the first, and again wears out as your opponent closes the gap.

You call another time-out and repeat the process. At this point, you are tired. Your opponent, who has stayed steady throughout, takes over and wins the game handily.

***

Relying on adrenaline at the beginning of a competition always becomes a stick in your spokes. It grinds you to a halt because humans didn't evolve with the ability to produce adrenaline for the full length of a competition. We evolved to sprint away from danger, which only takes a minute or two.

In short duration sports like the 100-metre dash, having a spike in adrenaline would be advantageous, but it is often difficult to time for the start of a race. Regardless of the sport, it's always best to come in with poise, and try to maintain that frame of mind for the duration of the competition. Even if you are the underdog, approach it the same way. Allow your opponent's fuel tank to run dry from the ups and downs of competition.

***

Those who have developed mastery of their mind say that their energy levels rise as they progress along the path to enlightenment. This energy comes from the balance they've established within.

The Buddha said, "When faced with joy or sorrow, the wise do not show elation or depression." So instead of jumping up and down whenever something good happens in sport, a better response is to give a fist pump on fitting occasions. Celebrations should come from *inner confidence*, not *outer confidence*. In other words, they should happen naturally, and not from a forced display of excitement. They should only last a second or two, at which point you should start your mental routine to prepare for the next action. Save the party for after the game, when the job is done.

STAY OFF THE EMOTIONAL ROLLER COASTER

If you find yourself getting swept away with the swings of your sport, keep in mind that even the best athletes in the world are susceptible to emotions.

In the 2022 Australian Open men's final, Daniil Medvedev squared off against Rafael Nadal. It ended up being a match that impeccably demonstrated the importance of having balance in the mind.

Medvedev won the first two sets and was nearly flawless up to that point. His focus was impressive; he never took his eyes off Nadal between points. And his balance was strong, giving an appropriate amount of celebration after copious winners. He was in complete control of the match.

At that point, Vegas odds gave Nadal only a 4 percent chance of winning the match.

In the third set, Medvedev lost his tranquility when the crowd started cheering his errors. In tennis, it's not proper etiquette for the crowd to cheer for mistakes (especially double faults), but when you are in a grand slam final against Nadal, who is usually the crowd favourite, you can expect it. Instead of accepting the situation for what it was and maintaining balance, Medvedev lost his cool and started taunting the crowd.

During changeovers, instead of using mental tools like slowing down the breath, he spent the entire ninety seconds berating the umpire about the unruly crowd. While he did this, he was getting his muscles worked on by the trainer. Is there something wrong with this picture from a mind-body standpoint?

Compare this change-over with an athlete like Novak Djokovic, who puts a towel over his head while remaining completely still. This is Zen.

Medvedev now had three opponents—the umpire, the crowd, and of course Nadal. While he was falling off the balance beam, Nadal was a mental fortress, delivering a mind-bending comeback by winning the final three sets of the match.

Nadal has won twenty-two grand slam titles for good reason. He knows the importance of keeping a level head through the emotional roller coaster that can occur in a grand slam final.

When you compete, be like Nadal—be unshakable.

LEAD WITH BALANCE

Sports create an enormous amount of energy that is felt by everyone, which is why we love competing so much. If you are the captain or leader of your team, it's especially important that you aren't susceptible to the emotions that will inevitably crop up during competition. You play an immense role with your team since negativity and over-excitement are contagious.

Lead with balance. Then your mates will have the appropriate level of arousal—not too high or too low. This doesn't mean being quiet and timid. It means staying absorbed, and using an appropriate tone of voice when speaking. Never hang your head when times get tough, or jump around in jubilation when things are going your way. Stay equanimous.

BE AN INTELLIGENT ATHLETE

Imagine for a minute that you are a high-performance athlete in ultimate. You have an upcoming game and as you drive to the field, you notice the wind is really howling. When you arrive, the wind is so strong it's practically blowing you over. At this moment, what's your mindset? Is it:

Oh my God, this is so ridiculous—how can anyone play in this?

Or is it:

This is amazing. I can't wait to throw a long bomb with the wind at my back!

The second mindset is better than the first; however, neither is optimal. The best mindset is a neutral one. In this case:

The wind is wind and it's the same for both teams.

With this mindset, you aren't blocking anything out. That would be resisting the wind, or pushing it away. This creates mental tension. Instead, spend a minute examining the wind in great detail. Do this by asking yourself:

Which way is it going?

Is it consistently blowing in one direction or does it swirl around?

Do we need to adjust our strategy because of the wind?

This is being an intelligent athlete.

TAKEAWAYS

➤ Our emotions are extremely fluctuant, so don't get hung up on mind-states such as *I struggle under pressure*.

➤ Remain equanimous to the emotions and feelings tied to sport. Watch them, non-judgmentally. In other words, acknowledge and accept.

➤ Stay balanced on the beam as you compete in sport by not getting down or reacting in over-excitement.

➤ Be mentally tough by quickly letting go of the good and bad that are bound to occur during sport.

➤ When you get in a rut, use phrases such as *water off a duck's back* to let go of the past.

➤ Don't rely on adrenaline. Start with poise, and maintain it throughout.

➤ Celebrate from a place of inner confidence, not an outward display of emotion that consumes energy and creates an emotional roller coaster.

➤ If you are the captain of your team, lead with emotional balance.

➤ Be an intelligent athlete by analyzing challenging situations.

9

RECHARGE

SILENCE IS A SOURCE OF GREAT STRENGTH

There are eighty-one Vipassana centres scattered around the world. Each one is strategically positioned away from noisy cities, but not so far away that transportation becomes a deterrent.

On my way to a Vipassana course a few years ago, I lost cell service, but luckily I had scribbled down the directions on a scrap of paper prior to departure. Several hills and missed turns later, there it was, in the middle of nowhere—a sign that read:

Quiet, please: meditation in progress.

Walking up to the front doors, I immediately felt more relaxed. I could feel the tension in my body start to release. This is the same feeling I get when I first arrive at my cottage, from the soothing sounds of birds chirping and the odor of pine and balsam trees.

Prior to the course, life was busy. My mind had been moving at the speed of light, except in circles instead of a straight line. My constant thinking, pondering, and strategizing around life was not conducive for focused meditation.

By the end of the course; however, my mind felt serene and my body rejuvenated. The silence had helped to settle my spinning brain, which was now moving in a slow, steady, straight line.

***

The day after the course, I was at home working on my laptop, catching up on a slew of emails. To my surprise, I was completely done in less than an hour. I didn't second guess any decisions, I just hit the reply button and typed a response. Prior to the retreat, I'd leave emails to simmer and stew in my head for days.

I not only experienced more clarity of mind, but had a spike in energy. When I went to the gym a day later, I pushed more weight than I had lifted in years! This is because "silence is a source of great strength" according to Lao Tzu, who is the founder of philosophical Taoism.

Author Yuval Noah Harari commits a full month every year to Vipassana because it gives him the direction and energy he needs to write bestselling books. Many years ago, I would have called a month (or even three days) of meditation a complete waste of time. Now, I understand that participating in a course is an investment of time that recharges our battery, making us much more productive.

***

Leading up to a meaningful competition in sport, it is valuable to find silence. You can do this by powering down your electronics and finding quiet space. In that space, do something that soothes your soul. This will give you energy.

REST IS A WEAPON

Jamie Kompon has been an assistant coach in the NHL since 2008. He is currently with the Florida Panthers, was previously with the Winnipeg Jets, and won a Stanley Cup with both the Los Angeles Kings and Chicago Blackhawks. Kompon understands that rest is a huge asset for his players, which is why he commonly writes on the team whiteboard:

Rest is a weapon.

***

To be at our best, we need the opposite of burnout, which is being fully engaged and absorbed. *Resting* puts us in that frame of mind. It's so simple, yet it's hard to be still. But when we find stillness, we recharge our mind and body.

MANAGE THE LOAD

Be careful paying a premium for tickets to watch
LeBron James play because he may be a healthy
scratch, especially if their team has already made the
playoffs and there's only a few games remaining in
the regular season. Lebron's coaches and trainers are
paying particular attention to *load management* so
that he can perform at his best in the post-season.

***

Overtraining and over-competing lead to a tired
mind. From that, we get easily irritated, which is
destructive to our performance. This can also lead
to burnout, where we simply don't want to show up
to practices, or even games. Therefore, managing the
load has become an increasingly important component of high-performance sport because athletes and
coaches are now realizing the power it can give us,
both mentally and physically.

LESS IS MORE

Kerry MacDonald is a volleyball coach and sport
scientist with a PhD in rest and recovery. He was
hired by the University of British Columbia's men's
volleyball program as head coach in 2016. In two
years' time, he took an average team and turned them
into national champions. Many people say it takes
five years to develop a program and win a national

championship, but Kerry was able to do it in just two because of his genius.

Halfway through their national championship season, Kerry lessened the load on his athletes by giving them an entire month off. They continued to take care of their minds and bodies, but no balls were bouncing in their gym because Kerry knew the value of time away from the court.

On top of giving his players ample time off, Kerry had each athlete wear a small device on their hip that recorded the number of times they jumped. Once a particular athlete reached a threshold, that athlete was either limited, or completely removed from jumping drills. This helped to manage the load because Kerry knows that jumping (and subsequent landing) sucks the juice out of his athletes.

In the national championship game, UBC swept the two-time defending champions Trinity Western Spartans in straight sets. The team looked energized and excited to compete. This was because Kerry is a sport scientist, meticulous when it comes to load management. It's a component of sport that we must address in order to flourish.

***

At one of his coaching seminars, MacDonald said, "Everyone's overtraining" when referring to the local volleyball community.

David Prissinotti, longtime athletic director at York House School, says, "Sometimes more is just more."

In many cases, *less is more*.

MENTAL AND PHYSICAL REPAIR

I learned the value of load management when I was coaching a team in the midst of a long and grueling season. We had seven tournaments scheduled, which is a heavy load for a season that's only three months long.

Our fourth tournament was a trip from Vancouver to Winnipeg. The tournament had a unique format. It was one pool consisting of eleven teams. We ended up playing ten round-robin matches, plus two playoff games, for a total of twelve matches in three and a half days. It was a lot.

We flew home late Saturday night, and when the athletes walked in the door for practice on Monday evening, I knew we needed a break. As the team began warming up, a few athletes came over to inform me of nagging injuries, while I overheard another athlete complaining about being really behind in schoolwork. I too felt drained, so decided to do something that was totally uncharacteristic of my coaching...

As practice was about to start, with the team dressed and ready, I called a huddle and asked everyone to have a seat. Once they sat down, I told them, "We aren't practicing today. In fact, we are going to take the entire week off with the exception of Thursday night's league game." They were stunned, since a week off in the middle of volleyball season was a totally foreign idea to them.

I gave them the following list of things to do for mental and physical repair:

Meditate.

Do breath-work.

Journal.

Stretch.

Massage, roll, release muscles.

Take a bath.

Drink plenty of water.

Eat lots of good food.

Go to bed early and/or take a nap.

Engage in a hobby.

The team walked away with a sense of confusion, but I could tell they were excited about having some extra time.

***

During that week, I repeatedly questioned my decision to cancel practices. I personally took the time to think and plan for the remainder of the season, which was valuable.

When we returned to practice the following Monday; however, I knew I'd made the right choice as soon as the team walked in the door. Everyone was happier, with a little pep in their step. A week before, there was excitement to rest, but now there was eagerness to get back to practice.

From that point on, our performance was excellent as we went on a twelve-game winning streak. In the thirteenth game, our season ended by losing a close five-set match, but it was an excellent finish to a great season. I'm certain we wouldn't have ended our season 12-1 if we hadn't taken that week off. The break replenished our energy stores, allowing us to jump higher and move quicker. More importantly though, our minds were refreshed, allowing proper mental functioning and the ability to make quicker decisions. Nowadays, the words *decision training* are popular in the sporting community, and we can increase the speed at which we make decisions by resting our minds.

TAKE A DAY OFF

One Sunday, I worked for my good friend Brian and his Smash Volleyball program. He had me lead three volleyball tryouts in a row. Swarms of athletes came in the door, and Brian asked our team of coaches to select the rosters by the end of the day. This was tough since we hadn't previously seen any of the athletes play.

After the last session, there was still paperwork and communication that needed to be done. All in all, my focus knob was cranked to high for about ten hours straight.

The following day, when I sat down to work on this book, my brain felt like it was going to explode. In the first few minutes, it simply would not function, not to mention that I felt physically exhausted. I tried to battle through, but got frustrated, so closed up my laptop. I tried again later in the day, to no avail.

My ability to write came back slowly over the next few days, thanks to impermanence.

***

On the following Sunday, I decided to do the opposite—absolutely nothing that required any brain power. My *day of nothing* was similar to a Sabbath day in Judaism and Christianity, where individuals are asked to take one rest day per week by following certain rules. To plan for my day, I googled *Sabbath day rules* and modified them to fit for me. The rules I came up with were:

No work.

No technology.

No driving.

No spending money.

No lights.

Take a minute and imagine a day where you implemented these rules. What would you do?

It's harder than it looks at first glance since it restricts many activities, particularly when we have to turn off our TV, laptop, and phone. What's interesting is that these activities require mental energy, and when they are removed, we become more vibrant.

Sure enough, on Monday morning when I sat down to write, everything flowed.

When comparing the two Sundays, I found there was a slight difference in the amount of physical energy required, but a sharp contrast in the amount of mental energy needed. This exemplifies how extra effort from our mind not only drains our mental energy stores, but our physical stores too. Mind and body are linked.

**

As you get close to a big competition, take a rest day to prepare your mind and body. It's important to not only take the day off, but to pay close attention to the things you do on that day. Make a list of rules that fit for you and your schedule, and have some activities ready, such as reading a book or going for a walk with a friend. If you get bored, tell yourself:

> *Boredom is a good thing. It will help me perform at my best.*

TAKE THE MIDDLE ROAD

We have to be careful not to get overly excited about this idea of rest since we want to enter into our final competition *in-practice*. I was guilty of this mistake one season of coaching. I cancelled a few key practices before the provincial championship and received a message back from our captain saying:

> *Why aren't we practicing today? I'm rested.*
> *We need to practice.*

I thought about it for a while, and she was right. Although we were rested, we weren't game-ready.

We finished that competition performing below our potential.

***

In Buddhism, there's an expression called *the middle road*, or *the middle way*, where action is conducted to avoid the two extremes. In other words, not too much and not too little.

In sport, we need to keep ourselves within this range by gauging our physical and mental readiness. The simplest way to do this is by asking ourselves questions like:

> *How do I feel?*

> *Am I excited to practice?*

> *Am I physically tired?*

Am I mentally drained?

Fatigue can greatly hinder our ability to perform, but practicing keeps our skills sharp. Finding the right balance between the two is truly an art… but it's the athletes and coaches who master this art that set themselves up for success.

PERIODIZE YOUR TRAINING

The Soviet Olympic weightlifting team dominated their sport in the 1960s. They broke numerous world records, some of which still stand. Their impressive surge was in large part due to a periodization model that was developed by one of their sport scientists named Leo Matveyev. He found a formula that properly balanced work and rest. Let's explore…

Matveyev's model is pretty complex, but we'll keep it simple. Basically, it tinkered with *volume* and *intensity*, where:

Volume is the amount that you practice.

Intensity is how hard you practice.

According to Matveyev, we want to train under high volume and low intensity at the beginning of a training cycle. As we approach our big day, we gradually flip these so our training regimen consists of a low volume and high intensity.

Tapering the volume toward the end of a training cycle isn't rocket science. Marathon runners have been doing this well before the Soviets started in the sixties. But what the Soviets introduced was an increase in intensity as the training cycle progressed. This would be the equivalent of a marathon runner doing a few short, fast runs leading up to a big race.

Building up to the Olympics, the Soviet scientists were meticulous with their record keeping, making sure each athlete had supreme energy and motivation to lift their personal bests. In the end, their results spoke for themselves. And later, their periodization model was translated into other languages and used in other sports.

***

One such sport is hockey.

In 2004, I was fortunate to have the opportunity to watch two NHL teams practice on game day. The contrast between the two practices was stark.

The Detroit Red Wings were in Calgary to play the Flames in game six of the 2004 Western Conference semi-final. The Flames were up 3-2 in the series. Each team had one hour of practice time and the visiting Red Wings were up first.

Throughout the scheduled hour, players came and went, doing various shooting and passing drills. Everything was laid back and unstructured. Some of the players didn't even put on their helmets.

This practice was characterized by *low volume* and *low intensity*.

Next up was the host Flames. They came flying out of the tunnel at the top of the hour and went straight into a few fast laps of the rink. Head coach Brian Sutter came onto the ice last and immediately tapped the boards with his stick. This signalled the team to break into the first drill.

A little while later, he tapped the boards twice and his troops broke into a second drill.

Finally, he tapped the boards three times and the team skated a few more fast laps before bolting off the ice.

The Flames practice only lasted about twenty minutes and the intensity could not have been any higher. It also had a sense of structure and intention.

This practice was characterized by a *low volume* and *high intensity*.

Sutter and the Flames coaching staff must have had knowledge of periodization. A short and sweet practice on game day fit perfectly in line with Matveyev's strategy, giving them the upper hand that night as they punched their ticket to the Stanley Cup final with a 1-0 victory over the Red Wings.

***

Leading up to a big competition, pay close attention to *how much* you practice (volume) and *how hard* you practice (intensity). That way, you'll achieve your personal best.

BE EXCITED TO COMPETE

At the time I learned about periodization, I was coaching a seventeen-and-under boys' volleyball team. I wanted to experiment with adjusting the load, especially since the club volleyball season can drag on. To do this, I started with long practices at the beginning of the season with a high number of repetitions. I also included strength-training sessions on Sundays.

As the season progressed, I softened the strength training, slowly cut down the length of practice, and lowered the number of reps by doing more game-play. I also encouraged a high level of effort during the game-play to raise the intensity.

Our last few practices before nationals, which were now only an hour and a quarter long, were excellent. I'd use the extra time to do mental training. A win-win situation.

Throughout the season, I was clearly explaining the concept of periodization to the players because I wanted them to know why practices and workouts were being diluted. I didn't want them to think that things were puttering out. The goal was quite the opposite—to ramp things up.

On the last day, I wanted feedback on the effectiveness of periodization, so we had a little discussion. The feedback was all positive. One athlete even said, "Usually, I feel run-down prior to nationals since the club season can feel long and drawn out. I'm usually tired, with thoughts of quitting. But not this year. I've never felt this excited for nationals."

This was the first time I put a significant amount of time and effort into altering the training schedule. It was a huge success. Since that experience, I make sure to have a periodization plan at the beginning of every season. I've learned that periodization truly works because by adjusting the volume and intensity, it puts us in an optimal state to perform when it's do or die.

BREATHE DIGITALLY

In James Nestor's popular book, *Breath*, Nestor researches various types of breath-work practiced in different cultures. He found one important commonality:

> *Slow down the breath, particularly*
> *the exhale.*

In his book, Nestor writes about Swami Rama, an Indian breathing master who is known to have incredible control over his mind and body. Rama has spent an extended period of time living and meditating in a cave. Stories say he's been found deep in meditation surrounded by crocodiles. How's that for facing fear?

When scientists studied Rama in a laboratory setting, he was able to consciously stop his heart from beating for seventeen seconds. Later, he topped this by creating a temperature difference of five degrees Celsius within two small areas on the same hand. Incredible!

***

The type of breathing Swami Rama endorses is a long, slow breath. Use the following steps to do what Rama calls his *2:1 digital breathing method*:

1. Lie down in Savasana.

2. Breathe in slowly through the nose using the belly, also known as *diaphragmatic breathing*.

3. Breathe out through the nose (again, using the belly). However long the inhale took, try to double it on the exhale. For example, if you breathe in to a count of three, breathe out to a count of six.

4. While counting, smooth out your breath so it is not jerky, noisy, or irregular.

5. Work to extend your breath to a count of fifteen seconds in and thirty seconds out.

Rama says it takes a long time to get to a thirty-second exhale. But once you do, he says, "you will feel like all the cells in your body are floating in the air." He also says, "you will have very good health… your memory will sharpen… and your skin will be as smooth as silk."

After I performed digital breathing for over a week, I'm not sure my skin was any smoother, but

I was able to extend my exhale. As a result I had a massive influx of energy. This is energy that can be used in sport. So try it out, because this tool will give you physical and mental stamina.

GET TO KNOW JOE

A good friend of mine, Steve, is the massage therapist for the Edmonton Oilers. He comes to town when his Oilers face off against our hometown Vancouver Canucks. I enjoy meeting up with him to get an update on recent happenings with the team and he always has a few good stories to share.

I once asked him what the players consume between periods. I was shocked when he said that many of them drink coffee and energy drinks, like Red Bull. I was surprised because I've drunk coffee before playing tennis more times than I can count and know one thing for sure: *if I drink coffee, I play poorly*. I feel jittery and my strokes are choppy. Also, my heart rate is high while my breathing is fast. Therefore, when I want to perform well, I drink decaf.

After meeting with Steve, I was reading Rafael Nadal's book when I came across a rule he abides by:

No caffeine on game days.

Later, in a conversation with squash pro G, he also mentioned that he avoids coffee on game days. Remember what G said, "I take a long, slow breath to reduce the number of thoughts." If he's right, and the speed of our breath is directly correlated to the number of thoughts we have, and caffeine increases our breath rate, then:

Caffeine increases thoughts.

Since a busy mind is not a reliable one, G drinks pineapple juice on game day and Nadal consumes plain pasta with olive oil. If you don't want to follow the advice of these masters of mind, then it's important that you run your own little experiment on this:

Before practice #1, consume strong coffee.

Before practice #2, drink weaker coffee.

Before practice #3, drink decaf.

Compare how you perform on all three days and repeat a few times to ensure accurate results.

***

A jolt of caffeine has many health benefits and can put us in a better mood. If you are someone that gets grouchy when you don't get your morning Joe, then consume enough caffeine to feel good, but be careful not to overdo it because it affects you psychologically and physiologically. Consuming the perfect amount of caffeine is an example of *the middle road*. Not too much, not too little.

Spend time getting to know Joe. Learn how he affects your mind, body, and ability to perform.

JUST ADD WATER

One of the easiest ways to restore your mind is by hydrating it. There's much debate on how much water one should consume per day, but many health experts recommend what's commonly known as the "8x8 rule." This is eight eight-ounce glasses of water.

***

On my trip to China to teach, I had a stopover in Beijing before continuing on to Zheng Zhou. When I got off the plane and went to have a drink of water from the fountain, I found it peculiar that there were two options—cold water and hot water.

When I got on the next flight, the majority of people on the plane were Chinese, and many asked the flight attendant for hot water. Also peculiar.

After a few days in Zheng Zhou, I saw hot water served in restaurants prior to meals. It was becoming clear that this habit is customary in Chinese culture.

***

A year later, I noticed one of my athletes (who is Chinese) drinking from a to-go mug prior to a game. I thought she was drinking coffee, but it turned out she was drinking hot water. She said, "My mom swears by it."

I tracked down her mom a little while later and she told me to be sure to drink it before competitions.

She said, "Make it as hot as you can handle and add a hint of ginger to calm your digestive system." She also said many of the oldest people in the world are from China and claim that the secret to longevity is to regularly drink hot water. Interesting.

After that conversation, I jumped on board. I started drinking hot water in the evenings and before playing sports. I don't notice much of a difference after one mug, but after two or three I feel a significant relaxation effect. Sometimes I get a strange pulsing feeling as if the tension in my body is melting away.

I certainly can't claim that drinking hot water will make you live longer, but I know from experience that it calms the nervous system.

Before a competition, be sure to get plenty of water into your system. Being hydrated will help you perform. Also, try hot water, to see if it helps alleviate your game-day jitters.

BREATHE AND BATH

Connor McDavid, currently the best hockey player on the planet bar none, takes hot baths to soothe his muscles and ease his mind. Based on the way McDavid is currently playing, we should do the same.

Here are a few tips to get the most out of your bath:

→ Take some deep breaths while in the tub. You'll find this combo is one of the ultimate stress relievers. You'll probably sleep like a baby that night, giving you even more energy the next day.

→ If taking a long bath, be sure it's at least a full day before your competition. If taken on game day, be sure to keep it short.

→ Saunas and steam rooms are another great option for body and mind. Again, keep it short on game day if you go with one of these options.

→ If a bath, hot tub, sauna, or steam is not accessible, take a hot shower.

→ Drink plenty of water and replace electrolytes while getting heat exposure.

→ Avoid cold showers and soaks before your big game. Use cold exposure for recovery.

Using heat, externally and internally, can truly make a difference in a competition because you come in with an advantage—a mind and body that are ready to rock.

TAKEAWAYS

➢ Power down your electronics to find silence before a competition.

➢ Take a full rest day leading up to your competition. If you'd like, make a list of rules for yourself.

➢ Find the right balance between being *rested* and *in-practice* by periodizing volume and intensity.

➢ Do *2:1 digital breathing* to recharge your battery.

➢ Experiment with varying amounts of caffeine prior to a competition. Find what works best.

➢ Drink one or two mugs of hot water with ginger on game day.

➢ Take a hot bath a day or two before your competition and combine it with deep breathing.

➢ Expose yourself to heat on game day but keep it short.

10

STAY POSITIVE

COMPASSION AND GRATITUDE

Recently, I was substitute teaching, filling in for a physical education teacher. I had two grade eight classes in the day and the lesson plan from the teacher was to have the students run a mile.

I began the first class by welcoming the students and giving them the plan for the day. The reaction from the class was one of horror, as if having to run a mile was the worst thing that had ever happened to them. I didn't push back and carried on with the class, bringing them outside to do three laps of the schoolyard. Overall, the effort was poor, the attitude was negative, and the complaining was relentless. The class ended with a debbie downer atmosphere.

In the next class, with the same lesson plan in hand, I knew I needed to do something different. So

I decided to tell them a story before going outside. It went something like this:

In a university class I taught a number of years ago, *principles of coaching*, I had a student that was born with cerebral palsy. He was unable to walk, so got around in a wheelchair. He had limited use of his hands, difficulties with his vision, and trouble hearing.

I met with him and his parents before the course started and his excitement to attend school was palpable. He was attending what he called "the university of life" since he wasn't interested in getting good grades, or any degrees. He just wanted to enjoy the experience of being at school.

For the first month or so of class, we didn't hear much from Luke, just random laughs that were three times as loud as everyone else's.

Then one day, Luke raised his hand with a question. I answered it and bounced a question back into his court, in hopes that he would speak to the class. Luke not only answered the question, but carried on for a few minutes, getting pretty deep into his life by telling us about some of the challenges he had faced growing up. He talked about how much he loved basketball and that he wanted to be a coach one day.

The last thing out of Luke's mouth remains with me to this day. He said, "I know that playing basketball is beyond my wildest dreams. The only thing I've ever wanted to do is get up out of this wheelchair and walk away."

Luke paused as you could hear a pin drop...

The class's over sixty students were frozen. In that moment, the compassion for Luke could be felt. In the next moment, we all looked at ourselves and became thankful for what we had been given—the ability to get up from our chairs and walk away.

I walked away that day with a lump in my throat thinking about Luke.

***

As I finished telling the story to the Grade 8 students, they were also stunned. They felt the same empathy for Luke that my university class had a few years earlier. I then told them, "We are going outside to do a mile run and today we are running for Luke. As you run, be thankful for your working arms and legs and the amazing brain that sits atop your body. It's not a race, just do the best you can and enjoy it."

When the class started running, I couldn't believe my eyes. It was a complete one-eighty from the first class. They ran hard, with smiles on their faces. They even cheered on the last few students to the finish line. It was a nice moment.

As we walked back to school, there was an over-arching feeling of positivity, and I even heard one student say, "That was awesome." It was awesome because they expressed *compassion*, which is the antidote for selfishness, and *gratitude*, which is the antidote for greed.

GRATITUDE FOR RESILIENCE

Saul Shrom is a former NCAA collegiate tennis player, now a mental performance coach. Recently, he began his own company called *Centre Court Mental Performance*, which provides a mental edge for athletes, businesses, and teams looking for sustainable high performance.

One group he is working with is the Capilano University men's volleyball team. First-year head coach, Darrin Moreira, introduced a gratitude circle before every practice and I was fortunate to be invited into the circle when I attended one of their practices. We connected the circle by touching feet with the athlete or coach on either side of us. Then we went around the circle so everyone could share what they were thankful for that day.

***

Later in the year, the team suffered their toughest loss of the season on the Friday night of a back-to-back weekend match-up against Columbia Bible College. They were anticipating a sweep, so there was unrest in the locker room after the game.

On Saturday, a few hours before the rematch, Saul led a group discussion and started it by asking, "Why do you think we practice gratitude every day?"

Saul informed me that although gratitude is beneficial for mental well-being and outlook on life, sometimes athletes may not understand how it is relevant to their performance. So it's important to provide some context behind this discipline.

The athletes discussed Saul's question and deciphered that the purpose of their gratitude circle was to train their minds to find positivity in tough situations. Saul agreed, adding to the discussion, "Some days, you may be in a good mood and when you arrive at practice, it's easy to think of something that you're grateful for. But on other days, you may have had a bad sleep the night before, struggled on a test that day, or argued with your partner right before practice. It's on these tough days that the gratitude exercise is especially powerful. Learning to find silver linings in adverse situations builds resilience on the volleyball court."

As the match began, Capilano came out firing. Whenever something troublesome found its way onto their side of the court, they were able to pick themselves up off the floor because of their commitment to gratitude. This resilience allowed them to play their best game of the year in a 3-1 victory.

I GET TO

Two up-and-coming coaches in Canada, Shane Smith and Donata Huebert, are commanding the Mount Royal University women's volleyball program. Shane, the head coach, and Donata, his partner and assistant coach, recently finished their first year coaching the team.

Shane is a good friend, and when I talked to him before the season started, he said, "We are leaving no stone unturned with this group." One of those stones is the mental side of the game.

An activity that Shane and Donata used to build positivity in their first year was to facilitate a discussion on the words *I have to* versus *I get to*. First, the athletes shared examples of things they had to do that day, such as go to class or study for exams. The mood in the room during that discussion was somewhat sombre, but that quickly changed when they switched to activities they got to do that day, like play volleyball.

Moving forward, *I get to* became contagious amongst the team as they began appreciating the good fortune they had been given to be a part of their team. This is gratitude, which is a concept that can be easily forgotten.

Come playoff time, Mount Royal shocked everyone in the Canada West playoffs by finishing third, earning a berth in the national championships.

At nationals, with their positive mental outlook, they continued their Cinderella story by plowing their way to the finals. Unfortunately, they came up one game short. And if it weren't for a key injury late in their semi-final game, they may have taken home the gold.

***

When we feel stuck in our sport, and treat it like it's work, we drag ourselves to practice. There is little enjoyment associated with this mindset and our performance collapses. This is an *I have to* mindset. But if we play our sport like kids in a sandbox, a smile gets plastered on our face and our level of performance goes up. This is an *I get to* mindset.

So ask yourself:

Do I have to or do I get to play sports today?

THERE ARE NO LITTLE THINGS

Legendary basketball coach John Wooden said to his players, "It's the details that are vital. Little things make big things happen." He also said, "Races are won by a fraction of a second, and national championship games by a single point. That fraction of a second or single point is the result of relevant details performed along the way."

Wooden's attention to detail is why he spent time at the beginning of every season teaching his teams how to properly put on their socks and shoes. It not only prevented the athletes from getting blisters, but taught them a valuable lesson:

Take care of the details.

***

I've watched my sister Colleen raise her son Ronin for the past twelve years. Every night, before Ronin goes to bed, she asks him for three good things that happened that day. This is an example of a little thing, geared toward ending the day on a positive note and a few good smiles. Although this activity may seem miniscule in the immediate term, these little jolts of happiness compound over time, growing into a mindset filled with positivity. Ronin has turned into a happy, fun-loving young man, thanks in part to his small acts of positivity every night before bed.

DON'T BE SELFISH

John Wooden also said to his players, "Don't whine, don't complain, and don't make excuses." These are selfish habits that we adopt from society; however, that doesn't mean we have to comply. We can choose a better way. Compassion is that way.

Zen monk Shunryu Suzuki said, "When our mind is compassionate, it is boundless." Compassion is developed in a Vipassana course. Each one-hour sit is actually an hour and five minutes. The extra five minutes at the end of the session is dedicated to *metta*, which is a form of meditation that's often referred to as *loving-kindness meditation*.

To practice metta, send positive energy, happiness, and goodwill to others. This is a tough exercise after sitting still for an hour, but by doing it routinely, we start to engender empathy toward those who are less fortunate. And it's important to send metta to *everyone*, including people we dislike. This dissolves selfishness.

UBUNTU

At the beginning of the Boston Celtics 2008 season, head coach Doc Rivers met a random woman who introduced him to the word *ubuntu*. Rivers asked her, "what the heck is ubuntu?"

She replied, "Go home and look it up."

Rivers was intrigued, so began researching it as soon as he got home. Within minutes, he knew the concept was a perfect fit for his team.

Ubuntu is an African way of life meaning compassion, and the belief in a universal bond of sharing that connects all humanity. It's the essence of being human. We are all linked and should learn from each other how to live. Nelson Mandela chose this way of life, preaching *ubuntu* as he joined hands with the South African vice president, who was a white man that once supported apartheid.

Rivers loved the concept of *ubuntu* because it not only brought his team together as one, but paid respect to their opponents. Rivers said in the docuseries *Coaches Playbook*, "I can never be threatened by you being good because the better you are, the better I am."

The Celtics rallied around *ubuntu* that season. In the end, they dismantled Phil Jackson's Lakers in game six of the NBA finals to take home the championship trophy.

***

Get to know your opponent and pay them respect. Once you see them as a friend instead of an enemy, you will feel less threatened by them and can perform to your full potential.

PROVIDE VALUE

Hall-of-fame basketball star Steve Nash averaged an astonishing 239 touches per game. No, this isn't the number of times he touched the ball, this is the number of times he touched a teammate. A statistician recorded this number, and the touches came in a multitude of ways, including high fives, low fives, fist bumps, and simple pats on the back.

Nash was once quoted as saying, "I believe that the measure of a person's life is the effect that they have on others." Because he had this belief, Nash clearly went out of his way to have a positive impact on his teammates. This fostered an environment of *cooperation* and *trust*, where helping one another was the mindset. This is why Nash won two NBA Most Valuable Player awards. He provided value.

DON'T GET STRANDED ON AN ISLAND

The University of Alberta Golden Bears men's volleyball team squared off against the top-ranked Trinity Western Spartans in the 2022 National Championship game. The Golden Bears won the first set, but you could feel the energy change hands when the Spartans crushed the Golden Bears, 25-12, in the second set. The Spartans had been doing this all year—starting slow and then trouncing their opponent. However, the ability to avoid negativity under adverse conditions is something that the Golden Bears had been working on since the beginning of the season.

After the Golden Bears lost to the Spartans in an exhibition game, head coach Brock Davidiuk had a realization—that a strong mental game would be needed to beat a team of this calibre. So he placed an emphasis on improving that area of their game.

To improve mentally, Davidiuk had sport psychologists attend practices to give his players immediate feedback. When an athlete made a mistake, Davidiuk's team of coaches and psychologists would look closely at their body language to see how they handled the mishap. If they showed signs of segregating themselves from the team, or what they called *getting lost on an island*, attention was immediately given to this athlete because this can be a slippery slope.

In order to keep everyone off the island, the coaches had each athlete write on the whiteboard the things they needed from their teammates in order to prevent themselves from *going internal* or *going into a shell*. Once on the board, each athlete could see what their teammates needed in tough times, whether it be a few words of encouragement or a kick in the ass.

The team also decided that forming a proper circle after every point, regardless of what happened, would help them remain united as a group. The circle was their mainland, preventing anyone from getting stranded on an island. Once their circle was formed, their three cues were to:

> *Smile.*

> *Give good eye contact.*

> *Support each other with reassuring words.*

Back to the national final. With their backs against the wall going into the third set, everyone on the Golden Bears was able to stay away from the island. Sticking together, they found their rhythm and won the third set.

They held onto momentum in the fourth set and were soon crowned national champions.

***

The lesson from this story is:

> *Negativity is a cancer and should be avoided at all costs.*

Find positivity by strengthening the solidarity with the people around you. The unity you develop will keep everyone mainland.

WRITE FREELY

When I began implementing meditation with the athletes that I coached, the benefits were instant. However, I soon learned that it wasn't for everyone. When we did our few minutes of meditation before practice, one or two athletes would sit there with their eyes open and fidget. I continued doing the short meditations before practice, since the majority of the team liked it, but I needed another method of introspection.

***

I first read about the idea of having a notebook for sport from ex-pro tennis player Brad Gilbert in his book, *Winning Ugly*. Gilbert carried a little black book in his tennis bag for taking notes on his opponents. However, I wanted to use our notebooks a little differently. Instead of taking notes on the opponent on the other side of the net, I wanted to take notes on the opponent on our side of the net—ourselves. Why? Because this is often the toughest opponent we face.

To introduce a sports notebook to our team, I went to the dollar store and bought each athlete a notebook and a pencil. I presented it to them as a little gift. They were intrigued because the idea of having a notebook for volleyball was uncommon. I told them that we would use it to *free write*, which meant that there were no rules. Each of them could write whatever they wanted. They wouldn't be required to share any of it with anyone else.

This is important for athletes to know because if they are writing words that are trying to fit a certain mould, the writing is not free. When they write freely, it becomes a mental surgery, but if they know someone else is going to read their words, the incision isn't deep enough.

Free writing is a similar tool I learned in the book *The Inner Game of Stress*, written by Timothy Gallwey, alongside doctors Edd Hanzelik and John Horton. A tool they recommend to examine anxiety is what they call a "magic pen." Although the writer uses a regular pen or pencil to write, the magic is created by letting the unconscious mind do the work. Instructions are to *write without thinking* or *just let the pen do the talking*. This can be a great way to unearth hidden contents within the mind.

I told my athletes a few more things before they started writing…

First, they could write about other things in their life outside of sport. In fact, this was encouraged, because the happenings in their lives have a considerable effect on their performance.

Second, athletes needed to know that there was no requirement for entries to be a certain length. If they had lots to write about, great, and if not, that was fine too. They should simply write what comes up, which helps the pen become more magical. If an athlete wanted something to write about, they could raise their hand and ask for a prompt. I had a list of questions ready, such as:

How do you feel?

What has been going well lately?

Is there anything getting in the way of your ability to practice/play? If so, what?

Do you want to make any changes?

What is your biggest fear?

What motivates you?

Who is the most important person in your life? Why?

What is your number-one goal?

What is your true passion in life?

***

Free writing is a tool that can lift the weight off your shoulders. Many athletes are turning to this mental tool because it's a powerful way to spill your guts to yourself. It tends to make peace with any anger or frustration because the mind empties what's inside, which is why many athletes claim they feel better immediately after writing. When negative thoughts get released from the mind, a plan can be made moving forward. Not only that, but when wishes are written down, they tend to manifest into reality.

KEEP YOUR GLASS HALF FULL

The other day, I biked to the store to get groceries. I loaded up my cart and was about to pay the cashier when I reached into an empty pocket. "I forgot my wallet," I said to her. "I'm such an idiot…"

I stared into space trying to remember where it was. "Aha," I said. "It's on my dining room table." I left the groceries behind and pedalled home to get it.

While biking, I was shaking my head and berating myself with negative self-talk for being so absent-minded. I did this unconsciously until I came to my senses. Once I became conscious of the negative thinking, I told myself:

> *Forgetting my wallet is a totally normal thing to do and everyone on the planet has done it at some point or another.*

This helped to slow down my negative thinking. A few moments later, I had another thought:

> *I remembered exactly where my wallet was in only a few seconds. Impressive.*

My outlook on the situation quickly went from a glass half empty to a glass half full, which is the one we want while competing in sport.

***

As a tennis coach that pays detailed attention to the mental side of the game, I've become fully aware of the negative self-talk (often in the form of profanities) that comes from the mouths of my athletes. I've heard self-talk words like *stupid* and *idiot* more times than I can count. When I hear these words, I step in immediately because this is a mindset void of confidence.

To start, I'll ask the athlete who their favourite tennis player is. When they name someone, I then ask, "Does that athlete ever hit the ball out of bounds?"

An immediate smile and sense of relief are always expressed as they answer back with "Of course."

I then ask, "Are they stupid?"

They usually have a chuckle and respond, "No."

My final question is designed to flip their mindset: "Tell me one thing you did well on that last missed shot."

The athlete is often confused by the question, taking a few seconds to come up with something. But in this moment, while they are searching for positivity, the mindset is getting flipped. As David Nurse says, "self-talk pivots from negative to positive."

The lesson?

> *Nobody's perfect in sport, so always keep your glass half full, no matter how bad it gets.*

SMILE

If you've never heard the name Eliud Kipchoge, you are not the only one. And if you can't pronounce it, you are also not alone. However it's pronounced, Kipchoge is the current world record holder for the men's full marathon, with an astonishing time of 2:01:39.

I ran a full marathon myself many years ago, and finished with a time of approximately four hours. The thought of doing it in about half that time is bonkers. In order to run a marathon at Kipchoge's pace, each mile needs to be run in about four and a half minutes.

One day, for fun, I decided to run a mile as fast as I could. I was sprinting, by my standards, and was completely exhausted in the last few strides. I came in with a time of just under six minutes—a paltry time in comparison to Kipchoge's mile. And he does it 26.2 times in a row!

***

To work through the pain of accomplishing a run of this magnitude, Kipchoge employs a strategy of forcing himself to smile, even though he's not overly enjoying himself. Researchers out of Ulster and Swansea universities studied smiling and its effect on running, and determined that smiling improves run times because athletes that intentionally smile utilize less oxygen. Even more interesting—the athletes that smiled perceived the run to be easier than the athletes that frowned, even though the run was the same duration and intensity.

Since smiling becomes deeply entwined with posi- tive events throughout the course of our lives, we can work backward by tricking our mind into perceiving an event is enjoyable by grinning from ear to ear.

HAVE JOY

Down at Kitsilano Beach, there is a string of beach volleyball courts. When the rainy season subsides in early spring, out of hibernation come the top volley- ball players in the province. From spring to fall, there are tournaments almost every Saturday and I enjoy walking the dog down to check out the action.

Although I am not much of a beach volleyball player, I can clearly see that the mental game is of utmost importance, especially since it consists of a full day in Mother Nature's elements. The sun, wind, and rain can make for a long and grueling day, with misery showing up pretty quickly with the wrong mindset. This mindset can become an ath- lete's nemesis, preventing them from performing at their best.

***

Dan is an athlete that stands out from the rest—not because of his incredible defense but because of his laid-back and seemingly effortless style of play. He understands that joy is the remedy for anguish, and therefore maintains a positive and easygoing attitude throughout the day. Because of his demeanour, he's the guy everyone wants to partner with. But Dan doesn't just choose the best player, he chooses the guy he'll have the most fun with.

Regardless of who Dan's playing with, it seems like he's in every final. If you were to speak with him afterwards, you wouldn't be able to tell whether he won or lost, since he'd be smiling either way.

JOY LEADS TO LOVE

Years ago, I attended a coaches clinic and will always remember a quote from the instructor. He said, "Kids vote with their feet." In other words, if sport is enjoyable, kids will come back. So youth coaches should place an emphasis on *having fun* in order to increase participation.

Having fun is not only applicable for kids and beginners, but adults and professionals. We all need to have fun, because if joy is absent, we won't want to go back.

***

Early in Phil Mickelson's career, he tried being quiet and blocking everything out; however, he quickly learned that these tactics were not effective. Mickelson now makes an effort to be more talkative, tell stories, and intentionally laugh. He does this because he knows it will make him looser and that, as a result, he will be more likely to find flow.

In Mihaly Csikszentmihalyi's book *Flow*, he states that, "Flow is a state of energized focus" and that "enjoyment is a precursor for flow." So to find focus, we must apply methods to enjoy what we are doing.

Over time, if we have many experiences of joy, it leads to love, which is why Mickelson said:

> *"I love golf beyond belief."*

FOR THE LOVE OF THE GAME

I've coached a few athletes over the years that were always keen and excited to practice. They were a pleasure to coach because of the cheer they brought to the court, day in and day out.

One such athlete is Emily; hers is another story worth telling…

When Emily first walked into the gym as a Grade 9 student, I remember thinking that she'd have a tough time making the junior team since it was mainly composed of Grade 10s. I was coaching the senior team at the time, which was made up of mostly Grade 11s and 12s.

When we met with the junior team coaches to determine rosters, it was not surprising that the coaches didn't plan to keep her. However, something inside me didn't want to let her go; I was worried that most likely this would be the end of her volleyball career. *She's such a nice girl,* I said to myself, *and would never cause any problems*. So, to everyone's surprise, I decided to take her on the senior team.

When I met with her to explain the situation and that she probably wouldn't get much (if any) playing time that year, she was ecstatic. I knew right then and there she'd be a good fit for our team, but I could never have predicted what would transpire over the next four years.

In her first year, as expected, Emily didn't get much court time, but was so excited to be a part of the team that she fell in love with volleyball. In the off-season, she played as much volleyball as possible and improved immensely.

Emily matured even more during her tenth grade year. She received court time at the end of the season following a few injuries. But unfortunately, she suffered a severe concussion early in our zone championship and was out for the rest of the season.

Earlier that year, after a tournament game, the coordinator came over to me with a player of the game award. It was a volleyball shaped like a heart, symbolizing the love of the game. I was told to give it to someone on our team. As soon as the coordinator placed the award in my hand, I immediately thought of Emily, even though she wasn't our best player that game. Nonetheless, in our post-game meeting, it seemed fitting to give her the award. When I handed it to her, she responded with, "Yes, I do love volleyball."

In her Grade 11 year, she not only made the starting roster, but morphed into a leader. She loved the mental training we did and would go home to practice on her own time. One day, she told me her "night before a game routine," which consisted of lighting candles and putting them on the floor around her as she lay down, relaxing and breathing. Her family thought she was nuts, but that didn't faze her because she knew it would help her perform the next day. Her love for volleyball trumped the perceptions of others. John Wooden said, "*Reputation* is who you're perceived to be, but *character* is who you really are." Emily clearly made this distinction.

In her graduating year, Emily took on an even larger role, moving into a key position on the left side. In her final game as a secondary student-athlete, she captured a provincial championship. About midway through the final match, she had a few attacks where she tried to be too crafty. As she came off the court for a time-out, she looked at me and said, "Mike... I gotta swing." I nodded in agreement.

She went back onto the court and smoked the next ball for a kill. I get shivers when I think about this moment because it displayed the confidence she had developed from four years of dedication to volleyball.

***

From day one, Emily was committed to improvement, more than any athlete I've coached over twenty-five years. She would film every game and go home to watch it, in detail. She did this because she knew she had to work twice as hard as everyone else because of the hand she was dealt. She played her cards flawlessly.

Emily is now playing post-secondary volleyball for Western University. If you'd told me that in her Grade 9 year, I'd have said *you're crazy*.

The moral of the story:

> *Never doubt anyone, especially if they have a love of the game.*

TAKEAWAYS

➤ Practice gratitude to build resilience.

➤ Send *metta* to everyone around you, including your enemy. This strengthens your compassion.

➤ Take care of the smallest details in your sport, because many little things add up to big things.

➤ Regardless of whether you compete in a team or individual sport, build unity with the people that surround you.

➤ Free-write by putting your thoughts on paper.

➤ Force yourself to smile. This keeps your glass half full.

➤ Place an emphasis on having fun, even on the biggest stage.

➤ Find love for your sport.

11

SEE THE BIG PICTURE

PROCESS VERSUS OUTCOME

One year, I was asked to step in to coach a Grade 9 girls' volleyball team. It was toward the end of their season, and due to unforeseen circumstances, the two coaches could not finish the season. So with two weeks remaining before the provincial championships, I agreed to take over.

The two weeks of practice went well and I felt like we were adequately prepared for provincials, but I wasn't sure what the competition would be like. At the end of our last practice, I had a formal meeting with the team. I asked how they wanted to approach the weekend and if they wanted to set any goals. One player responded with: "I want to win."

Another replied, "Me too."

A third said, "Same."

All their heads were nodding up and down in agreement. I then asked, "Is there anything else we want to accomplish this weekend?"

It was silent for a few seconds as the players looked at each other while shaking their heads from side to side. I was expecting a bit more of a discussion around this, but being the new coach, I didn't want to force anything. So we went into the tournament with the sole objective to win.

This is a *result-oriented goal*.

The tournament had a typical format for a provincial championship at that age, with a round robin on Friday evening followed by playoffs starting on Saturday morning. However, what was atypical in this championship was that all sixteen teams made the A side playoffs.

In the Friday evening round robin, we were absolutely awful. We got swept, losing all six sets. We finished last in our pool, ending the day with many of the players in tears since our vision of winning the tournament was now only a glimmer of hope.

When I got home that night, I sat down at the kitchen table to reflect on the disastrous round robin. I pulled out my collection of mental tools and did some thinking. I knew we needed to expand our goals to more than just winning, so I made a little slide show using 8x11 white paper. Each piece of paper contained a goal that I thought would be a good fit for our team.

In the morning prior to our first playoff game, we had a meeting. I was firm with my message and it went something like this…

"Do you remember the conversation we had at the end of our last practice? And how we set a goal to win this weekend?" Their heads nodded up and down, slowly this time. I continued, "Well, there are other reasons why we play sports. Don't get me wrong, winning is great, we all love it, and it certainly should be something we strive for. However, winning should be seen more as the icing on the cake and not the cake itself. So what is the cake? We play sports to be a part of a team and enjoy the camaraderie that comes with it. We play sports to work hard, learning to grit our teeth in the battles we face. This struggle builds character. We play sports to learn lessons that transfer over to our lives. One of those lessons is learning how to lose. These are only a few reasons. There are certainly more."

I carried on, "To win this tournament, we now need a miracle, so let's take a step back and modify our goals. I've come up with a few for us."

I took the slideshow out of my bag and began shuffling through the papers. "First, we are going to come together as a team. Let's be cohesive by supporting each other. Second, let's put forth a full effort today, doing the best we can. Then we can appreciate that good feeling at the end of the day. Third, play fearlessly today. Fourth, it's important we have fun by remaining positive, no matter what happens. And, lastly, be sure to learn something today, even if it's just one small thing. If we can do these things well, we will end the day satisfied, regardless of the place we finish."

These are *process-oriented goals.*

***

In our round of sixteen playoff match that morning, we drew one of the top teams in the tournament because of our poor results on Friday night. We started the game playing really well, but more importantly doing a good job of our new goals. We scratched and clawed our way to 23-23, but in the next point, our opposition's biggest hitter smoked a ball into the face of one of our defenders. Rattled, we lost the next point and set.

As we switched sides, with one of our key players tending to a bloody nose, adversity had reached its max. I walked into the team huddle and said, "Wow, that was awesome! You all played so hard and did such a great job of supporting one another." They all looked at me a bit confused, but it sent them a message—that winning wasn't the reason we'd showed up that day. I quickly showed them the slides, which got some optimism going.

We went back onto the court and played better than the first set, winning it by a handful of points.

Before the third and deciding set, I reminded everyone not to get too excited about winning, since that wasn't our priority, and to continue working on our new goals.

We won the third set and match. The positivity was now clearly felt amongst the team—something that was a few planets away the night before. Now, there was a glimmer of hope to have icing on our cake, but we needed to continue focusing on the cake.

Before our quarter-final match, I made sure to go over the slides again to remind everyone of our goals. We won that match in straight sets, playing even better than our first. Momentum was now really growing.

I showed the team the slides before our semi-final game and again we went out and won handily. Our snowball was massive.

Before the final, we were told we would be "in tough" since the team we were up against hadn't dropped a set all tournament. However, momentum is a powerful thing and our snowball rolled right over them.

This was a most unexpected provincial champion-ship, going from the doldrums of defeat on Friday night to the joy of victory on Saturday afternoon. In all my years of coaching and playing sports, I've never seen a turn-around of this magnitude in such a short period of time. It was mainly because we expanded our focus from the *outcome* to the *process*.

***

Winning should be a goal, there's no doubt, but be sure it's not the only one. Having other goals, and particularly ones that focus on the process, allows you to *see the big picture* of sport. This helps to answer the question:

Why am I doing this?

By answering this question, we remove the blinders that we often get toward winning. Ironically, once we eliminate our tunnel vision and see the entire field of view, we start to win.

BUILDING A HOUSE IS A PROCESS

Saul Shrom, one of our adept mental performance coaches, says, "Having a process mindset is massive." To strengthen this mindset, Saul says it's essential that the people surrounding athletes speak in a process-oriented way. Saul works with tennis players and ensures appropriate language is used by coaches and parents. He does this by providing a list of appropriate questions, phrases, and feedback that can be used with athletes. For example, a parent should ask their child questions like:

What were you particularly proud of in today's performance?

What did you enjoy about today?

These are much more effective than:

Did you win?

Saul teaches coaches and parents to focus on *growth* by using the analogy of building a house. Every time an athlete is presented with a comment, question, or feedback that is centred around things within the athlete's control (such as effort, decision-making, or following a game plan), a brick is laid. It takes time to build an athlete's house and their surrounding team plays an enormous role in helping to build it.

Week after week, month after month, year after year, everyone needs to prioritize growth; no matter what. Saul says it's easy to lose focus on the process when an athlete wins three tournaments in a row and then loses the fourth. The conversation can easily shift toward results, which is the equivalent of heaving large boulders at the athlete's house, causing hard work to come crumbling down. "It takes a long time to build a house, but not very long to break it down," Saul said. "So commitment and consistency from everyone are key."

***

As an athlete, it's your job to not only be process-minded, but to surround yourself with people who have a vested interest in you as an individual. Those people shouldn't be solely "in it to win it." Ignore those that try to throw rocks at your house by defining success differently than your team, such as the media, who only cares about your win-loss record.

If you keep building, eventually you will have a roof over your head with a solid foundation. It is at this point that sport becomes enjoyable and rewarding.

DETACH FROM WINNING

I've mentioned the name John Wooden a few times because he is a coaching legend. He's one of the most successful basketball coaches of all time, winning an unimaginable ten NCAA championships over a twelve-year period between 1964 and 1975.

Wooden knew the problems associated with the attachment to results, so never once used the word *win* during all those championships. The goal was to do their best each and every time they stepped onto the court.

Wooden, an English teacher by trade, was not happy with the dictionary's definition of *success*. It describes success as attaining *wealth*, *position*, and *power*. In response, he came up with his own definition to use with his team. It was:

> *Success is peace of mind attained by knowing that you did the best that you are capable of.*

Using this alternative spin on success, the young men under Wooden's tutelage learned the importance of effort, discipline, and hard work—while relaxing the grip on winning. This built well-rounded players.

***

A similar philosophy, in which the attention was taken off winning, was held by Bill Walsh. Walsh was the head coach of the San Francisco 49ers for three Super Bowl championships in the 1980s. He encouraged his team to focus on *learning*, and preached:

"The score takes care of itself."

***

Wanting to win is great; however, if we become obsessed, *pursuit* turns to *greed*. Shunryu Suzuki said, "If you are too demanding or greedy, your mind is not rich and self-sufficient." In the course of time, performance is impeded. Not only that, greed takes its toll on our lives away from the game. So loosen the attachment to winning by putting the spotlight on doing the best you can (like Wooden), or learning (like Walsh). This is a process-oriented mindset.

HAVE AN IDENTITY

When I was coaching a provincial volleyball team, we travelled to Edmonton to compete at nationals. The night before our first game, I met up with my buddy Steve, the massage therapist for the Edmonton Oilers. Whenever we meet, I always ask about the coaches, trying to get the inside scoop on the things they are doing with the team.

This time, he talked about an activity the Oilers were doing—*building an identity*. It was introduced by head coach Ken Hitchcock after winning a Stanley Cup with the Dallas Stars. Hitchcock claimed that the best dynasties had an identity made up of key words that defined them. He felt that identities were best described using three words. For example, the Philadelphia Flyers of the 1970s, also known as the "broad street bullies," could be described as *mean*, *rugged*, and *tough*. Every player that jumped over the boards with a Flyers jersey on played that way because this was the culture they built.

The Oilers were working on their identity with input from the players. The exercise forced each athlete to take a look in the mirror to see *who they currently were*, and *the direction they wanted to go*. Their team's identity hadn't been finalized at the time I met with Steve, but it was centred around *speed* and *agility*. The players were already working hard to improve those areas of the game.

***

When I went back to the hotel, I lay awake for hours because I realized that our volleyball team had been practicing and playing games for the past few months without any identity whatsoever. Everyone was playing their own style, since there was no discussion of *who we were*.

The next morning, I had breakfast with our assistant coach, Lindsey. I filled him in on what I'd learned from Steve the night before. I told Lindsey I wanted to implement an identity right away, before our first match. Since there was little time, I put him on the spot and asked him to come up with three words that distinguished us. He thought for a while, then said, "Scrappy." He paused again as he thought, then spat out, "Smart." Again he paused before saying, "Safe."

I scribbled down the three words, looked at them for a few seconds and replied, "Three S's, it's perfect."

A short time later, in our pre-game meeting, the team huddled in a quiet area outside the gym as I told them about my meeting with Steve and how Lindsey had come up with our identity words at breakfast. When I told them that our identity was *scrappy*, *smart*, and *safe*, they dug it.

I then said, "Let me expand... We are *scrappy*, meaning we do everything we can to keep the ball off the floor. We're gonna be *smart*, meaning we use our brains and don't do stupid things on or off the court. And thirdly, we are going to be a tough team to beat this weekend because we make few errors."

Now, our objective for the tournament was neatly laid out with process-oriented goals.

As the tournament got underway, we often wavered from our identity, trying to do things outside our reach. Before games, during time-outs, and upon reflection after matches, we would check in with our three words to keep us on track. If a player tried to hit a ball straight down, we could ask:

Was that smart?

Or if a ball hit the floor, we could ask:

Could you have gotten that ball up?

Questions like these were nudging them to play according to the mould of our identity. If an athlete did something that was scrappy, smart, or safe, it was rewarded—regardless of the outcome of the point.

After a good quarter-final win, we found ourselves in the semi-finals against Team Alberta. The buzz throughout the tournament was that Alberta and Ontario were the two best teams by far, and that everyone else was playing for bronze. I made sure to tell the team that *anything is possible*, especially if we stuck to our identity.

We ended up playing incredibly well, losing 15-13 in the fifth and final set. It was funny—although we lost the match, it didn't have that losing feeling. In fact, it had a winning feeling. This was because we nearly beat a team that was far more talented than us on paper. And we achieved our goals of playing scrappy, smart, and safe.

We won the bronze match and walked away with smiles on our faces and a sense of pride. There's no doubt in my mind that using the identity tool gave us the guidance we needed in that tournament to stay on the rails. The instructions were clear…

Do these three things well and the score will take care of itself.

***

Take a minute to create an identity for yourself in sport, or other area of life. Start by brainstorming a list of words that might fit. Once your brain is tapped out of possible words, condense it down to the three that you like best. You can have more than three words, but keep it simple by not asking too much of yourself. If you can't think of three, be patient—words will come to you as you continue competing. Feel free to substitute words, since your original three are certainly not written in stone. This is an ongoing process, and is an important exercise because it will help you answer the question:

Who am I?

CORE VALUES

Steve Kerr is arguably the best shooter in NBA history, retaining the honour of having the highest three-point shooting percentage of all-time. While playing for the Bulls, and under the guidance of Phil Jackson, Steve learned the importance of having access to words in the locker room. Now that he's the head coach of the Golden State Warriors, he uses the words *joy*, *mindfulness*, *compassion*, and *competition* as a set of "core values" to make these concepts more urgent.

Between 2014 and 2018, the Warriors squared off against the dominant LeBron James and the Cleveland Cavaliers in four consecutive NBA finals.

Using their language, in the form of core values, they captured three of the four championship rings.

Steve Kerr and Phil Jackson are extremely successful coaches because they value the mental component of basketball. Because of that, we can learn from them. Their message?

> *Use words that have meaning to guide us on our journeys.*

LET GO OF LOSING

A long time ago, so I've been told, hunters created an ingenious way of catching monkeys. They built wooden pots that could hold a banana inside, with a small hole carved into the side of the pot. The dimensions of the hole were perfect for a monkey to fit their hand in, but not big enough to allow them to pull the banana out with a clenched fist. As the hunters approached the traps, the monkeys had the opportunity to let go of the banana, pull their hand out, and run away. But instead, they refused and got caught. Their minds were so fixated on the banana, they just couldn't let go.

This story sounds ridiculous at first since it seems too logical for the monkeys to let go of the banana. But when we humans take a step back from life, we see that we also have trouble letting go. When we lose in sport, for example, it can be very difficult to move on. However, releasing a loss from our mind is essential in order to continue pushing forward.

***

Dawn Staley has been the head basketball coach of the South Carolina Gamecocks since 2008. In that time, she has built the program from the ground up. Along their way to being crowned national champions, Staley noticed that her players were having difficulty letting go of losing. They wanted to win so badly that they couldn't move on after a defeat, and it was affecting the way they played in future games.

To help her athletes let go of failure, Staley explained that an important step to becoming a champion is losing. She asked them to accept it and learn from it. This process should only take a day, so she instituted a *twenty-four-hour rule*. By her rule, athletes could agonize over a defeat for twenty-four hours, but once that time was up, it was back to work. This was enough time for them to reflect, but not dwell, and allowed them to continue pushing forward on their quest—one foot in front of the other.

FAIL FORWARD

At times on our journey, we will have setbacks, but if we use these difficult times as learning experiences, we maintain persistence.

Nelson Mandela once said, "I never lose. I either win or I learn." This is called *failing forward*, where defeat is not seen as a loss, but as a step in the right direction. This is characteristic of an individual or group with a growth mindset—always growing, never stagnant.

USE PRESSURE AS A PRIVILEGE

In 2007, the Boston Celtics pulled off a blockbuster trade for big guns Ray Allen, Kevin Garnett, and Paul Pierce. Head coach Doc Rivers now had a load of pressure on his plate, along with his athletes, since the Celtics now had more than enough talent to win a championship. The drug that Rivers used to put their pressure into perspective was in the form of words. Those words were:

> *Pressure is a privilege.*

In *Coaches Playbook*, Rivers said in a team meeting, "Who wants to go their whole life without a pressure situation?" When no hands went up he added, "OK, so instead of running away from pressure, let's run toward it. Let's accept that it's hard and enjoy that challenge. When we are confronted with pressure, understand that we worked hard to get there. We earned it, so let's embrace it."

***

The day after I watched the show, I was in a pick-up tennis game and was confronted with a pressure situation. Our opponents held serve to go up 5-4. As we were switching sides, my inner dialogue went something like this…

> *Crunch time, hmm, who's turn is it to*
> *serve?... Damn it, it's mine.*

As I finished the self-talk, I caught myself. I was trying to run away from the pressure of serving, hoping it would land on my partner's shoulders.

I quickly changed my course of thought by reciting Doc's three mantras:

> *Pressure's a privilege.*

> *Run toward it.*

> *Embrace and enjoy the challenge in front*
> *of me.*

Almost immediately, I felt more confident and proceeded to hold serve.

So many times in the past, I'd get beat in that situation because I wanted to run away from the pressure. But not this time, since there was an instant boost in confidence that resulted from re-framing the meaning of pressure.

***

Relish the pressure that lands on your shoulders because if you are the top gun, you clearly worked hard to get there. That's an honour and a privilege.

MANAGE EXPECTATIONS

Our squash pro, G, explains that playing with expectation can be analyzed using an arrow. If you are playing with an *up arrow*, then you are entering a competition as the underdog. Either that or you've found a way to manage your expectations. You typically perform better with this up arrow because the pressure to win is under control.

Things become more challenging when you play with a *down arrow*, which is being the favourite, or holding on tightly to the expectation to win. In this situation, you usually have a hard time performing.

To become more aware of your expectation arrow, ask yourself a few questions:

Is my expectation arrow going up or down?

If it's going down, how heavy is it?

If it's heavy, where is the weight coming from?

If you've concluded from these questions that you have a heavy down arrow, make a list of all the individuals or groups of people that put pressure on you. Then quantify how much. For example:

Myself: 25%

My team: 25%

Strangers (fans/crowd): 25%

Dad: 15%

Mom: 10%

In the situation of this athlete, they've determined where their expectation is coming from. Now, they can spend time deciding who they want to play for.

Maybe this athlete decides that they'd be content playing for *themselves* and their *team*. If that's the case, this athlete should frequently remind themselves of this. Their mantra could be:

I play for myself and my team, and that's it.

The athlete should ignore judgements from others outside of their circle by developing thick skin toward their negative comments. They should tell themselves:

I don't care what they say because I don't play for them.

Even congratulatory comments from strangers are nice to hear, but shouldn't get soaked up by the ego. They should say:

Satisfying the wishes of people outside my team isn't why I play.

The weight of this athlete's arrow slowly becomes lighter. They are then able to perform at an elevated level because they have an answer for the question:

Who do I play for?

PERSPECTIVE

Providing closure on a season or career helps with the big picture. It is an exercise that's often overlooked. Either we forget, are too lazy, or don't see the value in it. I'm guilty of all three of these over the course of my playing and coaching career. It is, however, necessary to take time to reflect on the journeys we embark upon. It's also valuable to look ahead to the new directions we are headed.

***

Phil Jackson knew the importance of providing closure. At the end of their last dance season, Phil arranged a team meeting and asked each athlete to write down and speak a few words about what it meant to be a part of their dynasty.

In the meeting, after each athlete read their words aloud, Phil collected the papers, put them in a tin can, and turned the lights out. He then lit a match and tossed it in the can as the team watched their profound words go up in smoke.

Steve Kerr said this was one of the most powerful moments of his life. It signified the end of an era, and the burning memories implied that the past was gone. It was time to move on to the next chapter in life.

***

As a coach, I've tried a few different ways to provide closure for athletes. Formal meetings were effective, but it seemed like they never went as planned. And I quickly learned that I didn't have the magic touch of a Phil Jackson.

I also tried having individual meetings. Although these were very beneficial, they were difficult to set-up with our busy lives and were extremely time consuming with many of the meetings going on for hours.

Although these methods failed, I've now found a method of closure that works, and the idea came from another legendary coach named Phil...

I was five-foot-nothing in Grade 10, so most coaches looked past me. Except for one, Phil Hudson, who took me on his club volleyball team and later on his high school team. For many years, he taught me the skills of the game—but more importantly, the skills I needed for life. After I graduated high school, he got me into coaching right away, which ended up being a huge part of my life. He also recommended me for the teaching position I held for thirteen years at the University of Winnipeg. I often look back and wonder where I'd be if I didn't have Phil as a mentor.

For closure, Phil would hand each of us an envelope at our last practice of the season. He would ask us to wait until we were at home before opening it. Inside was a letter written by Phil that concluded our season. It was spoken from his heart, which we rarely saw during the chaos of the season. I appreciated the extra mile he went to give us a proper ending, particularly in my graduating year. It forced me to stop, think, and look back on all the fond memories of high school sport. It also gave me a chance to ponder the future, with excitement about what was around the corner.

Now, as a coach, I write letters to my athletes to provide them closure at the end of a season. Writing the letter allows me to deliver the right words to wrap-up the year. It is not only well received by athletes, but provides me value in writing them. It's a nice opportunity to sit and think.

Whether it's writing a letter, having team or individual meetings, or any other form of closure, it's a part of sport that should not be overlooked because it provides *perspective*.

FREEDOM

Roger Federer says, "I'm at my best when I'm up 40-love in a game because I can play free." When up 40-love, Federer has a more relaxed and confident demeanour that gives him the freedom to go for shots.

Another way to find freedom in sport is by having things in perspective. To do this, take time to think, which will give you the answer to the questions:

Who am I?

Why do I play?

Who do I play for?

Being able to answer these questions will provide you context, which removes the chains that prevent you from excellence. Once removed, you can play your sport, and live your life, up 40-love.

TAKEAWAYS

➤ Be sure to have both result- and process-oriented goals.

➤ Build a team of people around you that isn't solely focused on winning. Ensure the language is centred around development and progress.

➤ Create an identity using two to four words that reflect how you want to compete.

➤ Spend a short amount of time reflecting after a defeat, at which point let it go and continue moving forward on your journey.

➤ Have a growth mindset where you continue to learn and grow, regardless of whether you win or lose.

➤ Pressure is a privilege, so embrace it.

➤ Make a list of all the people that put pressure on you. Quantify how much pressure each is contributing. Then decide who you want to play for.

➤ Take time to step back from your sport to see the big picture. This will provide perspective, resulting in freedom.

CONCLUSION

PLAY YOUR CARDS RIGHT

Imagine the collection of mental tools in this book are a deck of cards. Each card represents a mental skill that you've trained leading up to your big day. If you've trained well, you have easy access to a number of cards, which become particularly handy during moments of pressure. Here's how to play your cards in those situations…

You can't play all your cards at once, since your mind can only focus on one thing at a time. For that reason, you'll have to play your cards in sequence. For example, you can first opt to play your confidence card by puffing up your chest and reciting your mantra to yourself. In the next moment, you can take a long, slow breath; mentally resetting and loading your muscles. Finally, you can use your eyes to focus intently on the task, silencing self-talk.

The three cards you've chosen to play are:

Confidence.

Breathe.

Focus.

This will set you up for optimal performance. There is no guarantee that things will go *exactly* as planned, but you've prepared yourself well.

On the contrary, if you let fear take over, forget to breathe, and fail to narrow your focus, no amount of physical training will enable you to perform in this situation. As a result, it's unlikely you will get the outcome you wanted.

***

On some days, you will be missing a key card. This makes it difficult to perform at your best. Here is an experience I had with missing a card...

Prior to a tennis tournament match, I felt like I was going into the game with my mind on point. Feeling fully prepared and ready fifteen minutes before game-time, I got a call from Angie in panic. She had taken Rudy off-leash near the tennis courts and couldn't find him. I ran over, frantically searching for him in the woods while screaming *Rudy!!!* at the top of my lungs. After several minutes of screaming his name, he popped out of the bush and we put him back on leash. I ran back to the courts just in time for the start of the match.

In the warm-up, I was breathing heavily and my hands were jittery from the jolt of fear Rudy had given me. Because *fear trumps confidence*, the unpredictable event stole the confidence card I was ready to play twenty minutes earlier.

Not surprisingly, we went down 4-1 early in the match, which was a pro-set up to nine games. I was able to regain some confidence as the match wore on; however, I wasn't able to find my rhythm and we lost the match.

After the game, the other cards in my hand became valuable. I was able to maintain the balance of my mind, stay positive, and keep perspective on the situation by understanding that some things are out of my control. That night, I reflected, which helped me get back to regular life the next day. This is the twenty-four-hour rule.

On the contrary, had I succumbed to negative emotions, mental instability, and failure to see the big picture, I'd wrestle with this loss for days.

***

If you didn't before, you now understand the importance of training your mind for sport. What's more, once you gain access to these mental skills through sport, they translate to life away from the game. Whether it's working on a group project, writing a book, or preparing yourself for public speaking, the mental skills in this book will allow you to thrive in all facets of life. They will get you to the highest level in anything and everything you do.

The Buddha said, "Indeed, not by any means of transport, such as elephants or horses, can one go to the place one has never been before; but by thoroughly taming oneself, the tamed one can get to that place."

That place is Nibanna, or enlightenment.

The End

ANATOMY OF A WELL-DESIGNED MENTAL PREPARATION PLAN

BUILDING UP TO COMPETITION

- ➤ Grow your meditation practice.
- ➤ Learn various forms of breath-work and choose the one that works best for you.
- ➤ Improve your mindfulness during daily tasks.
- ➤ Practice eye-work.
- ➤ Visualize positive outcomes.
- ➤ Make a highlight reel of your best moments.
- ➤ Develop a mental routine.
- ➤ Find a role model, watch them perform, and replicate their actions in practice.
- ➤ Build grit by doing things that are difficult.

- Use the scaling tool to raise awareness of certain mental components of sport.

- Create a mantra statement.

- Periodize your training schedule.

- Write about what's on your mind.

- Construct process-oriented and result-oriented goals.

- Create an identity.

- Know *why you play* and *who you play for*.

DAY BEFORE COMPETITION

- Have an agenda of exactly what you will do to prepare for the next day.

- Spend time sitting or lying down to calm your mind and relax your body.

- Discuss with someone on your team, or write in your journal, about how you are feeling.

- Visualize yourself performing well.

- Watch your highlight reel.

- Recite your mantra statement.

- Meditate.

- Spend a few minutes watching your role model.

- Take a bath while taking some deep breaths.

> Drink hot ginger water in the evening.

> Keep your mind busy before bed with activities like colouring or reading.

DAY OF COMPETITION

> Plan out your morning.

> Be mindful of your caffeine intake.

> Drink hot ginger water.

> Do an activity like yoga that promotes movement, breathing and focus.

> Perform breath-work such as *2-1 digital breathing*, the *Wim Hof technique*, or *lion's breath*.

> Warm-up your eyes.

> Watch your highlight reel.

> Spend a few minutes watching your role model.

> Recite your mantra.

> Acknowledge and accept your feelings without reacting to them.

> Get heat exposure with a shower, sauna, steam or tub. Don't overdo it.

> Take a magic minute.

DURING COMPETITION

➢ Always stay in the moment. Use anchors like your breath and vision.

➢ Power down your focus during breaks in action but remain present.

➢ Use your mental routine, guidance-talk, and a reset cue between actions.

➢ Accept distractions, then re-focus.

➢ Look for quiet moments. Be still, aware, and enjoy them.

➢ Stay in mental balance by letting go.

➢ Stay off the island.

➢ Support your teammates with high-fives.

➢ Smile.

AFTER COMPETITION

➢ Take time to think and reflect.

➢ Limit your reflection time to twenty-four hours after competition.

➢ Have a growth mindset, regardless of the outcome.

➢ Provide closure if you are at the end of a season or career.

➤ Stay involved in sport, because it's what we live for.